Developing Personal, Social and Moral Education through Physical Education

For years physical education has been viewed as being instrumental in developing personal and social characteristics. The theoretical and historical nature of this contribution has received some attention, but the practical applications of what teachers can really do has been largely ignored. This book redresses that balance by providing teachers with practical advice so that physical education can be used as an effective vehicle for the all-round personal development of the individual.

Material in four main sections in this accessible and timely book include:

- A focus on curriculum development, planning units of work and lesson planning
- Practical ideas and applications to promote the affective development and physical skill development of pupils
- A consideration of different types of assessment and suggestions on which forms are most appropriate for measuring programme effectiveness and the personal development of pupils
- A close look at the role of the reflective practitioner and a framework within which teachers can reflect on their practice

Developing Personal, Social and Moral Education through Physical Education provides teachers with the opportunity to extend and develop their abilities in teaching their subject. It also promotes physical education as a subject that has continued relevance in the twenty-first century.

Anthony Laker is the Degree Director of Physical Education in the Department of Exercise and Sport Science at East Carolina University. He is the editor of the *Journal of Sport Pedagogy* and the author of *Beyond the Boundaries of Physical Education: Educating Young People for Citizenship and Social Responsibility* published by RoutledgeFalmer.

Developing Personal, Social and Moral Education through Physical Education

A Practical Guide for Teachers

Anthony Laker

London and New York

First published 2001 by RoutledgeFalmer
11 New Fetter Lane, London EC4P 4EE

Simultaneously published in the USA and Canada
by RoutledgeFalmer
29 West 35th Street, New York, NY 10001

RoutledgeFalmer is an imprint of the Taylor & Francis Group

© 2001 Anthony Laker

Typeset in Melior by RefineCatch Limited, Bungay, Suffolk
Printed and bound in Great Britain by St Edmundsbury Press, Bury St Edmunds, Suffolk

British Library Cataloguing in Publication Data
A catalogue record for this book is available from the British Library

Library of Congress Cataloging in Publication Data
Laker, Anthony, 1951–
    Developing personal, social and moral education through physical education: a practical guide for teachers / Anthony Laker.
        p. cm.
    Includes bibliographical references and index.
    1. Physical education and training – Social aspects – Great Britain – Case studies.
    2. Physical education and training – Moral and ethical aspects – Great Britain – Case studies.
    I. Title
    GV342.27 .L26 2001   00–050997
    613.7′07′041–dc21

    ISBN 0–7507–0929–4 (pbk)

Contents

CONTENTS

Chapter 3
Assessing   54

The Theory   **54**

The Practice   **62**

A Case Study   **79**

Chapter 4
Reflecting   82

The Theory   **82**

The Practice   **85**

A Case Study: Reflective Practice and Action Research   **93**

Illustrations

Tables

Figures

Acknowledgements

Figure 1.3 redrawn by permission from Anthony Laker (1996) 'Learning to teach through the physical, as well as of the physical', *British Journal of Physical Education*, 27 (4): 18–22.

Figure 3.2 reproduced and adapted, by permission, from *The Affective Domain in Physical Education*, Curriculum Support Series, developed by Joan Halas. Copyright © 1989 by Manitoba Education and Training, Winnipeg, Manitoba, Canada. All rights reserved.

Figure 3.4 redrawn by permission from James R. Whitehead (1995) 'A study of children's physical self-perceptions using an adapted physical self-perception questionnaire', *Pediatric Exercise Science*, 7: 132–51.

Introduction

The purpose of this book is to enable teachers to teach physical education in a way that encompasses social and personal development. That, simply put, is what makes this approach different. The physical side of the subject is not, nor should it ever be, ignored, but this different approach balances the multiple outcomes of physical education so that *all* the recognised, potential benefits can be achieved. This is particularly relevant now because of recent government initiatives, but it retains its relevance much longer than for here and now. A school subject that can contribute to social and personal development, as well as to cognitive and, of course, physical development, is a rarity in the school curriculum. For this reason, we must retain control of our subject and exploit it for the benefit of all.

Personal, social and health education (PSHE) and citizenship are very much on the agenda of the educational establishment, and indeed on the agenda of the government. As well as reading, 'riting and 'rithmetic (the three Rs) there are now two more Rs: Respect and Responsibility. This is not the place for a critical analysis of why this is occurring now, but it is an opportunity for physical education to move to the forefront in developing these areas of the curriculum. It is an opportune time for physical education to develop and promote a postmodern pedagogy that is inclusive, pluralist, eclectic and empowering for pupils and for teachers. Physical education has a long history of claiming to promote affective behaviours in participants, and a wealth of recent research supports that idea. This book takes that research and applies it in practical situations.

The introduction of citizenship into schools and the new framework for PSHE (QCA, 1999a) make these issues pertinent. Now is the time to embrace all the research and philosophical debate and to transform school physical education into a subject for the twenty-first century. By adopting an eclectic pedagogy that is holistic and philanthropic in nature, physical education can at last fulfil its potential and become a key subject in the school curriculum. If we continue to rely on the purely technocratic interpretation of physical education that has been predominant for decades, we are not releasing the potential of our subject. More importantly, we are short-changing our pupils, our future citizens, by giving them only one manifestation of a multifaceted subject. Not only that, but we are neglecting to use physical education to develop and educate their complete *selves*.

Physical education has much to offer its participants, but it is a subject that suffers in comparison with many other school subjects. The worth of physical education is in danger of being devalued. It is not 'academic'; it's only about 'playing games' – these are frequent criticisms of the subject. Teachers of the subject, and teacher educators, need to work together to raise awareness of its potential. Those of us involved in the subject know that it is worth more than its present currency, and we need to be part of its evolution into a subject that fulfils its potential in being relevant and worthwhile. In this way we can produce a subject that contributes to the personal and social development of our pupils and enhances the promotion and understanding of citizenship in our communities.

Teachers are faced with many constraints on their time. However, it is important to make time to promote the subject, thus raising its value and thereby the status of the participants, the teachers and the subject in the educational hierarchy.

Universities, colleges of education and institutes of higher education have been training teachers for many years. These institutions have done their best to produce excellent teachers by using research from the education community and applying it in their teacher training courses. In the main, this has worked out quite well. Of course, there have been complaints and voices have been raised when the best intentions have not always delivered what they promised. Hence the frequent attacks on 'wishy-washy liberal' teachers, and the beginnings of emancipatory education from the 1960s. This was followed by a similar attack on physical education teachers in the mid-1980s supposedly for being anti-competitive, anti-sport and too 'politically correct'. According to the media, our teachers were entirely to blame for the failure of our national sports teams! But in spite of these isolated instances, the training institutions have, in general, produced very good teachers.

We know from the research what talents and characteristics are needed for a teacher to be effective in educating pupils. However, because of the nature of most of the research, which is experimental, positivist and scientific, the trend has been very much to focus on the technical side of teacher education. It has been assumed that teachers of physical education are there to educate pupils physically, to train them in physical skills, to get them and then keep them fit, to make them into the best participants of sports, games and physical activities that they can be. We know what to do to improve skills and induce fitness, and much of our curriculum is based on the notion of skill development and performance.

What we have is a multi-activity, performance-based curriculum within which the teachers apply their education in trying to produce skilled, fit performers. Physical education is education *of* the physical. This has been the accepted face of the subject for many years. But there are alternative views and many curriculum documents, educational texts and authoritative writers have presented these alternative views. This book attempts to join that company and presents a different way of looking at physical education, a different way of teaching the subject and a different way of measuring the outcomes of that teaching.

We have a pluralistic society and that is reflected in our education system, or rather it is reflected in the individuals, the children, in our education system. There are many different types of child in our schools and each child has many different needs. A different approach is required to meet those different needs. The different approach proposed here is an attempt to address some of those needs with a new, philanthropic pedagogy set within an already established framework.

A Different Approach

This different approach is simply that physical education has much more to offer than just the education of the physical part of a person. The following are some of the outcomes that are variously claimed for physical education and sports participation:

- physical, competitive, sporting
- responsibility, community, citizenship
- spiritual, moral, ethical
- emotional, caring, affective.

Obviously, this is by no means a complete list of potential outcomes, but the suggestion here is that physical education can contribute to our physical selves, our emotional, social and personal (or affective) selves, our spiritual selves, and our community selves; in short, physical education should contribute to the development of the *whole* person. Physical education has the potential to make a real contribution in other areas of an individual's educational development. This view is well supported by curriculum documents, physical education texts and current research (Hellison, 1985; Laker, 2000). In spite of this recognition of multiple contributions, the educational establishment and physical education in practice have, to date, only paid lip service to these expanded possibilities. The approach and methods described in this book are different in that they place the personal and social components in the foreground along with, not instead of, the physical and the cognitive.

What makes this approach different is that it does not privilege any one aspect of physical education over any other. It recognises that all have equal importance, if not necessarily equal weighting. The National Curriculum for physical education (NCPE) in England and Wales states that the greatest importance should be attached to the performance aspect of physical education and this must therefore carry the most weighting. Having located this work in the NCPE, and recognised the restrictions that this places on curriculum development and teachers' freedom of choice, it is also important to acknowledge that what is recommended here can be applied in a variety of curricular settings and contexts, and is not constrained by geographical location.

The physical nature of the subject is what sets it apart and gives it such potential, and it would be foolish and self-defeating to deny that or to try to usurp that. This physical nature is part of the strength of physical education. And this strength is enhanced by the broad appeal of the subject and of course its broad potential. It is fairly easy to identify a range of affective characteristics; these are traits like positive attitude, cooperative behaviour, humour, independence, enjoyment and self-esteem. Recently, there has been a reawakening of the notion that schools are not just for educating children and training them for adult life, but that the educational process has a responsibility to produce rational, effective, socially responsible citizens who can adopt a fulfilling and useful role in their community and society. Education is now being charged with producing responsible citizens.

Citizenship and Social Responsibility

Citizenship has a long history of being on the educational agenda. In fact, the Greek city states required fit young men for the military and an educated populace to take an effective role in citizenship. Increasing concerns about apathy and the cynicism being expressed about political and public life have again pushed citizenship to the forefront of the educational debate. There are also worries about 'disaffected youth'. These are youngsters who perceive that education and school have very little relevance for them in their everyday lives. (For those readers interested in this area in particular, I can recommend Hellison, 1985 and the *Journal of Physical Education, Recreation and Dance*, 1993.)

As a response to these concerns, the Crick report (QCA, 1998) identified three strands that partially constitute what it is to be a citizen. First, there is moral and social responsibility; secondly, there is an element of community involvement; and thirdly, political literacy is deemed desirable.

Social and moral responsibility fit very well with the rationale for using physical education as a vehicle for the promotion of PSHE. Society clearly wants young people to know right from wrong, to have a deep-seated sense of fairness and to value a moral code that facilitates living together as a community.

Sport, as a microcosm of society, can help with this inculcation of values. Children can be taught that playing by the rules allows a game to take place for everyone's benefit. What is consciously promoted in physical education can be transferred into other areas of the curriculum and into young peoples' lives in general.

Crick recommends that children learn about their neighbourhoods and their local communities. Schools do not exist in a vacuum, they exist in a community context. Many schools are community schools and provide a variety of services for the local community, from the provision of adult, and continuing, education classes to the provision of expertise and recreation facilities. Children can also learn at school that there is a global network of sporting communities. A girl playing soccer at a primary school in England shares a similar experience with that of a boy halfway across the world who is also playing soccer, except that it is in the foothills of the Himalayas. Being part of a sporting community also provides a wealth of common experience that is shared by people wherever sport is played. People of similar interests and shared experiences have a common ground that can be transformed into communication.

The third strand of citizenship, political literacy, is a little harder to identify in school sport and physical education. Obviously there are political initiatives in education and some of these are manifested in physical education; the existence of specialist sports colleges and an emphasis on activity performance are just two such examples. Older pupils can certainly be made aware that there is a political dimension to sport as part of their studies. It is also possible to find examples of politics and sport being unavoidably intertwined, as in the violent and political disturbances at the Olympic Games. For all our protestations about the purity of sport, it cannot in reality be seen as separate from the real world – and politics is part of the real world.

Being a rational citizen is part of being a socially responsible member of society. Part of the increased value being placed on citizenship is illustrated by the objective to educate and produce problem-solving, enquiring individuals who are able to work independently, and with others, for the greater good; who are able to exercise freedom of expression and choice in a socially and democratically just society; and who take individual and collective responsibility for themselves, the community and society in general. Many of these aspects of citizenship are now being claimed as objectives of school sport and physical education.

The Layout

This book is a practical guide for teachers, but it is not a prescriptive 'cookbook' that tells you 'how to do it'. The purpose of the book is to alert you to possibilities and to provide a practical framework for implementing the different approach presented here. The proposals are based on solid research and grounded in the theory of effective teaching and learning. Throughout the book, I have cited instances of research in the case studies to illustrate that these ideas work. Not only do they work, but their effects carry over to other areas of school life, benefiting the individuals and institutions in many contexts. However, I would not presume to say 'This is how it must be done'; I am more comfortable saying 'This is how it could be done, try it and see.'

The book is organised into chapters so that you can easily identify what information is most relevant to you and access it accordingly. Each chapter begins with a quick look at the theory behind the practical applications. Following this are the practical suggestions for teachers to consider in their day-to-day teaching. Some examples of best practice are used to highlight how these suggestions can be incorporated into physical education programmes. Lastly, relevant case studies and reports of research are used to show that this approach really does work.

Chapter 1 deals with the planning process. The curriculum planning has already been done in the NCPE, but the values that underpin the curriculum will be examined. Practitioners need to be aware of a variety of values and educational objectives if they are to share in the delivery of this new pedagogy. There will be suggestions and examples for you on how to plan for the affective development of your pupils. Lesson plans and units of work are the tools of the teacher's trade in the planning phase, and these will be looked at to see how they can be adapted to take account of an expanded delivery of the subject.

Implementation of this planning is the focus of Chapter 2. This deals with the practical applications of this different approach. Learning in the personal and social development domains can be improved by using some of the suggested methods from this chapter. The teaching strategies presented in Chapter 2 provide you with a starting point from which to devise and implement your own ideas. Many of the frameworks can be adapted for use in a variety of different scenarios and settings. This resource should be the catalyst for teachers to develop their own teaching, to take full account of their talents and to enhance their physical education programme delivery.

In Chapter 3, we will look at the thorny issue of assessment. We know how to assess performance and cognition, but the assessment of the affective is much more difficult. There is a review of the possibilities of using the various types of assessment that are available. Many assessment techniques, however, require lengthy procedures that are totally inappropriate in very busy schools. This chapter concentrates on some assessment suggestions and implementations that can be achieved without too much disruption or extra work for the teachers involved.

Lastly, the value of reflecting on one's practice is discussed in Chapter 4. Most teachers evaluate their lessons. Even if this does not have a formal manifestation, there is usually a consideration of what went well in a lesson and what did not go quite so well. Reflection is somewhat different, in that one's total pedagogical stance is scrutinised. This is obviously not done after every lesson, but it needs to be done periodically to ascertain one's professional development. In this way, the suggestions here for reflective practice match in very well with a requirement for the continuing professional development of teachers.

Chapter 1 Planning

THE THEORY

The Curriculum Process

Because England and Wales have an NCPE, a large degree of the planning process is removed from the practitioner and located in the hands of the politicians, albeit through their working parties and consultations. But if we want to add an extra component into the existing curriculum we need to know how to establish a rationale for that component, and how to implement it.

Most curriculum planning includes a lot of backward tracking questions. What do the children need to get from this subject? What is the end product of education supposed to be? What part will our subject play in contributing to that end product? And so on, and so on. The crucial question in that selection is: What should be the end product of education? Various theorists will have a number of answers ranging from 'Education is there to reproduce a stable society, to maintain the status quo' to 'Education is for social control, it represses, stratifies and turns children into useful members of the production chain.' But let us take a more altruistic and benevolent point of view. Let us say that we want young people to have the opportunity and encouragement to fulfil their potential, thereby becoming rational, thinking members of our society who can contribute to the common good in a number of ways, including demonstrating individual, cooperative and environmental responsibility. The next step is to ask what qualities, skills and knowledge will children need to meet this suggested educational outcome. It seems that to achieve potential, which is a commonly quoted aim for education, a wide-ranging, comprehensive curriculum must be in place that is inclusive, not only in its provision for a multiplicity of groups, but also in the delivery of all the subject components. So,

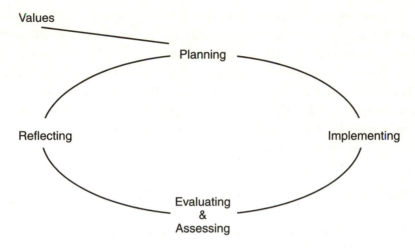

FIGURE 1.1   A cyclical model of curriculum development and planning

in a somewhat roundabout way, we are saying that, in educating our children, we must make sure that they receive all that the subjects have to offer in order for them to be able to develop their full potential. In a needs-based curriculum, this naturally includes developing cognitive abilities, physical abilities and the social and personal characteristics that are the province of this book. Some would say that the contribution of physical education is limited to developing physical abilities, but enough has been written and recognised to know that this is only part of the subject's contribution.

A model for curriculum development that allows a reflective process to occur and feed back into the planning process would be a cyclical model, as shown in Figure 1.1. This model has been constructed to match the chapters of this book. For detailed information on each of the model components, readers should refer to the specific chapters. However, a brief description of each of the components and how the model works as a dynamic entity will enhance the understanding of the interrelatedness of the whole process.

What is important?

Before any programme can be successfully put in place, the people who will have to implement it must believe in it. The programme and the practitioners should share the same goals and values. The goals and values that are embedded in the NCPE and in the guidelines for PSHE have already been formalised and a programme to improve the personal and social development of children fits well within those remits. Specific curriculum goals are based on the notion of providing opportunities for each child to reach their full potential in all areas of their development. This is one of the common values in most programmes of educational provision. This value has been translated into a workable curriculum which espouses certain aims, for example promoting spiritual, moral, cultural, mental and physical development and preparing children for the opportunities, responsibilities and experiences of adult life. These broad statements provide strategic directions that schools must follow. As mentioned earlier, delivering and interpreting the curriculum are very much in the hands of individual departments and teachers, so any discussion of goals and values must be aimed at a practical, contextual level.

What do we want to achieve?

The first part of the process has already been done for the schools and teachers who have to implement the curriculum. The values held are clearly stated in the outcomes and purposes of the National Curriculum and in the subject-specific orders. The second part of the process is the planning of the educational experiences. These experiences have, to some extent, already been selected. The subjects that constitute the National Curriculum have been chosen by the government using their working parties and consultation committees. But individual schools, departments and teachers can still have some influence in this part of the process. There is some freedom to decide how these subjects are organised and planned to provide an effective curriculum. On a school-wide basis this is reflected in how the timetable is structured and how much time is given to each of the subjects. Although subject to government regulations and recommendations, these decisions rest mainly with headteachers and senior management in schools. However, once a subject has been allocated its place, it is usually the responsibility of individual departments to implement the requirements of the National Curriculum for their subjects. The organisation of physical education, its delivery and its assessment are the areas in which teachers can have a major influence.

How are we going to achieve it?

It is at this second stage – planning – that teachers can establish a rationale for the way physical education is to be taught and can also plan in detail the way it will be implemented to address that rationale. The establishment of a rationale should not be problematic, for much of the work has been done for us. Many writers have established aims and purposes of physical education and all have included items from the affective and social domains (Jewett and Bain, 1985: 119–59; Underwood, 1983: 39–44; DFE, 1995: 2). One of the most recent, Casbon (1999), says that physical education should, among other purposes, help children discover their physical and personal selves and also develop relationships with others. Physical education does not need any more rationale than that already in existence. Teachers must therefore put forward the case for social and personal development with some degree of vigour. Fortunately plenty of material is available to be able to do this effectively.

When it comes to planning the delivery to take advantage of physical education's potential in social and personal development areas, and also the effectively argued rationale, it is the integration of the new with the existing that is crucial to the success of the enterprise. Given that it would be impossible in the current educational and political climate to create a curriculum based solely around the notion of affective development, teachers will need to consider some of the strategies recommended by Hellison and Templin (1991: 115–20). The first of the proposals for building a curriculum is to build a framework within which values are developed into activities. In their example, Hellison and Templin use a fitness framework based on the value of a healthy, active lifestyle. This is adapted to accommodate an additional emphasis on motor-skill development and responsibility because the planning teacher values these aspects of pupils' development. In our situation (i.e. with an NCPE in England and Wales) we do not really have the freedom to start from scratch in this way. The values that are reflected in the NCPE are clearly defined for us.

Hellison and Templin's second suggestion is something called the 51 per cent rule. In this scenario, there is an existing curriculum model that reflects values and decision made by others, possibly administrators and parents. The best that the teachers can hope to achieve would be to add on as much of their favoured model as possible, leaving at least 51 per cent of the existing programme intact. We certainly have a curriculum model in place that dictates to a large extent what is taught. Even if it were desirable and teachers wanted to, they could not reject up to half of a mandatory curriculum model. As mentioned before, there is hardly enough time as it is to teach all that they are required to teach.

The third way of creating a curriculum is to select key components from the existing models and incorporate them into an eclectic whole. So a teacher might decide that the personal development of an adventure-education model and the health benefits of a health-related exercise model are the most important components to include in a physical education curriculum. This is not too dissimilar to the NCPE. There is the central core of a multi-activity model with a few components such as dance and outdoor and adventurous activities added on. This third suggestion, therefore, has possibilities for consideration.

Hellison and Templin (1991) mention one further approach to planning that is already in use in the curriculum in England and Wales. Its adoption as a method of promoting personal and social development should, therefore, be fairly easy. This approach is the use of cross-curricular themes. Hellison and Templin are strong advocates of this thematic approach. They suggest that 'personal–social development values, such as fair play, can become themes . . . and probably ought to if the teacher wants students to learn them' (p. 119).

A theme is a concept or group of concepts, a set of values, a series of ideas and notions ideologically linked to form a coherent whole. In our curriculum in England and Wales we have five cross-curricular themes of health education, economic and industrial understanding, careers education and guidance, education for citizenship, and environmental education (National Curriculum Council, 1990). It can be seen that within each theme there could be many contributory elements. Education for citizenship could include awareness of the democratic process, political literacy and some notion of the historical background to government. Health education could include health-related exercise (HRE), personal hygiene and nutrition. In a similar way, affective development, or personal and social development, is made up of many components.

The example we can usefully look at is the way health-related exercise is taught in the NCPE. As it stands, HRE is not an area of activity or part of the multi-activity model that is in place. Instead, HRE is a central part of the cross-curricular theme of health education. Health education can be related to any subject in the curriculum, but HRE is associated with physical education. It can be taught either in dedicated units of work, or alongside other NCPE subjects in a way that integrates the content of the cross-curricular theme and the subject. Some schools might, for example, teach a unit of work on diet and weight control. This would stand on its own as a discrete unit of work, although good teachers would certainly try to make connections across the curriculum. However, the preferred recommendation is that such content would be better dealt with as a theme, possibly by linking it to aspects of human biology, nutrition and the benefits of physical activity in weight control.

There are proposals in place to replace health education as a cross-curricular theme with PSHE (QCA, 1999a). This means that although the guidelines and recommendations for implementation are non-statutory, the teaching of the theme will have to take place. This is provided for in the umbrella requirements of the Education Reform Act of 1988 that state that 'all state schools . . . provide all pupils with a curriculum that: is broadly balanced; promotes their spiritual, moral, cultural, mental and physical development; prepares them for the opportunities, responsibilities and experiences of adult life' (School Curriculum and Assessment Authority, 1996: 3). It will not be a National Curriculum subject, but it will be a part of every school's curriculum. This is much the same way that religious education and sex education operate in the school curriculum.

Many schools already operate programmes of personal, social and moral education. The proposals provide a framework that schools can adopt if they wish. How they teach the theme will be left up to individual schools to interpret. This presents physical education with an opportunity that should not be missed. Here is a situation where academic theory represented by the work of

Hellison and Templin, political action represented by the adoption of PSHE as a theme, and education for the benefit of the children by maximising a subject's potential, are all united in harmony.

Let's put it into practice!

Having achieved the considerable planning necessary, teachers then have to implement the curriculum. This is the crucial teaching and learning phase of the process. Much is known about effective teaching. How teachers perform in the sports hall and on the sports field is informed by a large body of research literature. Exactly *how* teachers teach will have a large degree of influence over their success when it comes to promoting affective development. There will need to be some adaptation of traditional methods and some adoption of various teaching strategies designed specifically for personal and social development through physical education. Teachers have a major individual influence over this stage of the curriculum process. This is the interface between teaching and learning, the point at which a change in behaviour can be brought about; this is the essential pedagogical moment. Much of a teacher's education and training will have been conducted with this moment in mind, the moment when a teacher stands in front of a class and teaches children physical education.

As has been mentioned earlier, there is a clear understanding of what an effective teacher is. We know what teacher behaviours encourage the learning of psychomotor skills. This part of the process, the implementation of these new ideas and this different approach, needs some new teacher strategies. In short, the teacher needs a larger 'bag of tricks' to attain the achievement of affective aims. Chapter 2 deals with this in detail and will help teachers fill their 'bags of tricks'. However, good practice in teaching remains at the heart of any suggestions made here. The foundations of knowledge of subject, planning, a love of the job, respect for children and good classroom skills do not change. In this regard, many readers will be well placed to take advantage of the proposed eclectic, philanthropic pedagogy.

Did we achieve what we set out to achieve?

As with all teaching, there must be a system of evaluation and assessment to determine the effectiveness of the curriculum as a whole, and also the effectiveness of the teaching itself. This is the point in the process where we put our curriculum and our teaching under the microscope. In the earlier stages of planning the curriculum, we will have said what we hope to achieve. Simply put: Did we achieve it or not? Did our pupils become more independent, or did they show signs of caring for each other, or did they become more aware of some

Have student behaviours, whether or not stated as behavioural objectives, progressed in the direction of the programme goals?

Have instructional strategies that are clearly related to the implementation of the programme goals been employed on a daily basis?

What are the teachers' and students' perceptions, thoughts and feelings about the programme?

(Hellison and Templin, 1991: 144–5)

FIGURE 1.2   Some questions to aid programme evaluation

of their responsibilities as citizens? The programme must be measured against the original objectives. Ways of assessing and evaluating pupil progress in these affective dimensions are dealt with in Chapter 3. But these are specific suggestions for assessing pupil progress, not ways of evaluating a complete programme.

Hellison and Templin (1991: 144) comment that programme evaluation is the type of evaluation least likely to occur. To enable this unlikely evaluation to become more likely, they provide three simple question for teachers to ask of their programmes (Figure 1.2). The answers to these questions will tell teachers whether their pupils (students) have improved in their psychomotor development and affective development, whether the teachers have taught as they said they would teach, and what pupils and teachers think about the programme. Such a broad evaluative mechanism allows teachers to determine whether the teaching and learning have been a meaningful experience and ultimately whether there is anything that needs to be changed.

The results of the assessment will determine what happens in the next step in the curriculum development cycle. This progress towards a judgement that might result in change leads into the reflective phase, which in the curriculum development cycle is closely related to feedback.

How can we do better next time?

Much has been written about 'the reflective practitioner' and 'reflective teaching'. What it is to be that 'reflective practitioner' is dealt with in Chapter 4. Although this stage of the cycle has an element of reflection, it is more about feedback and programme improvement. Naturally there is an element of reflection in that process: How could we improve the future without reflecting on the past? Reflection in this sense means 'taking account of' or 'learning the lessons from' what has gone before.

If all has gone well and the programme is working as we expected it to work, if objectives are being met, and teachers and pupils are happy with it, then there is very little reason to change anything. On the other hand, if things did not happen as expected, or the objectives have changed, or teachers or pupils are unhappy with the programme, then there will need to be changes. The assessment and evaluation phase will have highlighted what the problem areas are and these changes need to be planned into the programme before it reaches the implementation phase again. The most common time to do this is at the end of the academic year, and on an annual basis. This allows the next implementation phase to begin with a new academic year. And so the cycle of curriculum development continues.

THE PRACTICE

It is common practice to plan work in physical education programmes in *schemes of work*, *units of work* and *lesson plans*. Schemes of work are long-term planning documents usually covering periods of time such as a single key stage (two, three or four years). In a school working within the NCPE there would be a scheme of work for each area of activity (Games, Gymnastic Activities, Dance, Athletic Activities, Outdoor and Adventurous Activities, and Swimming). Because of the long-term nature of schemes of work, and the fact that they are closely linked to the overall curriculum document (in most cases in England and Wales the NCPE), it is unlikely that much in the way of social and personal development will be included in them. Schemes of work ensure the continuity of provision and coherence of the physical education programme. They are important from a structural standpoint in that they provide overall frameworks of subject development.

Units of work are able to cater for specific objectives and they typically cover a more limited period of time, such as a half term, or a whole term. Units of work give an outline of the content to be covered in that topic during that time span. So there might be units of work for Year 3 Gymnastics (one half term), Year 8 Soccer (one whole term) and so on. Psychomotor, cognitive and affective objectives are stated on unit documents. Each unit of work would show how work is planned to meet these objectives and how this contributes to making realistic progress in achieving these objectives from week to week.

Lesson plans obviously cover individual lessons and are much more detailed than either schemes of work or units of work. Lesson plans explain the activities that will be done in the lesson, how those activities will be organised, and teaching points that will be used. Teaching points are those key bits of information that are crucial to learning; they are also cues to jog your memory! There will also be a statement of lesson objectives, again in the psychomotor, cognitive and affective areas. Most lesson plans will also have some administrative details, such as number in class, resources needed, how progress will be evaluated and so on. Lesson plans tend to be more individualised in that you can develop your own style that works for you and is specific to you. As such, there is more room for individual input and adaptation.

It will be apparent from the preceding explanation of schemes of work, units of work and lesson plans that the planning components that can most effectively accommodate personal and social development aspects of physical education are units of work and lesson plans. We now look at how this can work in practice.

Units of Work

The first step in practical planning is to decide what *characteristics* are to be targeted. In this regard, we are looking at personal traits from the affective domain of physical education. A long list of traits is a fairly unwieldy item and is therefore of little use in planning or delivery. Figure 1.3 groups traits together under generic headings, so *cooperation* includes teamwork, helping each other; *sportsmanship* includes such traits as fair play, honesty and respect and so on. This grouping makes them more easily manageable when it comes to devising teaching strategies for the promotion of the traits.

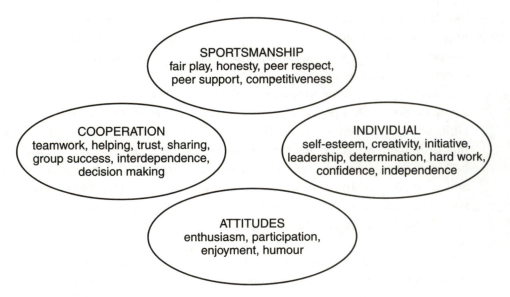

FIGURE 1.3   Generic groupings of individual traits

Teaching strategies can now be considered. Certain strategies will be more effective than others in promoting the desired traits. In general terms these strategies fit into three categories:

- Teacher talk, discussion, restatement of objectives
- Modelling of behaviours by teacher and pupils
- Reward systems, reinforcement, praise.

The selection of which strategy to use will depend upon a number of factors such as age of the children, existing strategies in use in the school, teacher preference, type of activity and so on. For example, it might be more appropriate to use reward systems with younger children than with older children. The prospect of 16-year-olds being excited by the award of a gold star is hard to imagine! Chapter 2 contains a number of teacher strategies that can be incorporated into the planning of units of work. Of course, it could be that you will want to use different strategies at different times in the unit. Teacher talk and restatement might come at the beginning of a unit, laying out the expectations and the way the new approach is going to work. Modelling and demonstration of the selected traits or behaviours could be more appropriate during the main body of the unit, culminating with an award ceremony to bring the unit to a close.

Because of their nature, certain sports activities lend themselves to the promotion of certain personality traits. The selection of activities to achieve specific outcomes is an important consideration for teachers in the construction of their units of work. On a very simplistic level it can be argued that team games help cooperation, teamwork and so on, and that dance and educational gymnastics promote creativity, self-control and so on. Therefore, the importance of taking into account the nature of different sporting activities needs to be fully recognised. As well as activity selection being crucial, the way an activity is organised has a large bearing on the achievement of the lesson objectives. Volleyball would seem an ideal sport to use to encourage teamwork, but when practices are organised on an individual basis it somewhat loses this potential. So even if the activity itself was appropriate, the way in which it is organised is important for the development of affective outcomes.

Planning is central to success during teaching and it is necessary to consider all these factors as they relate to each other. These considerations raise combination questions (Figure 1.4).

The example unit of work included here (Table 1.1) shows the result of this planning process. At the top of the plan are the administrative details; area of activity, key stage, year in school, unit title and number of lessons in the unit. Below these details are the objectives, both psychomotor and cross-curricular, that you and pupils will work towards. The psychomotor objectives should be taken from the overall curriculum document that the school is using; usually in England and Wales this will be the NCPE. The cross-curricular objectives will reflect the established ethos of the school or department and will be derived from the school's or department's adaptation of the framework for PSHE (QCA, 1999a). Each lesson in the unit is indicated horizontally across the plan. Down

TABLE 1.1   Unit of work

Area of activity: Games		Unit title: Ball control	
Key Stage: 2		Year: 4	

Lesson structure	Lesson 1	Lesson 2	Lesson 3
Introduction	Intro unit, explain cross-curricular strategy and element 'Follow my partner'	Restate cooperation 'Aim for the day' 'Simon Says' – stretches, jog	*Key words* on board 'Help, aim, dribble' Jump lines on floor
Development	*Individual* Throw, catch, bounce, catch Against wall Ditto in *pairs*	*Pairs* Passing and control (catching) with feet Still → moving *4's* Think up game for 4 using kick and catch/control	*Individual* Move ball with hands feet dribble *4's* Drills for dribbles coach ⎱ ×2 scorer ⎰
Conclusion	2 v. 2 Passing and catching game	Kickball games	Dribbling relays Feet, hands
Cross-curricular element: Cooperation Helping Being positive	*Pairs work* 'Take care with each pass' 'Help partner' Stickers	*Pairs* Reciprocal work *4's* Helping strikers	*Teams* Cheer for team, help with hints Stickers and status for certificates

Resources needed	Assessment criteria
Variety of balls Variety of bats, rackets, unihoc sticks Cones Bibs or braids Benches and mats	Physical element assessed by teacher observation and skills circuit results Affective element assessed by stickers chart (ipsative) and certificates (summative)

Time (lessons × mins): 6 × 40 mins

Objectives   *Prac* – Perform effectively in activities requiring quick decision making. To improve aspects of ball control
    Aff – To improve cooperation by helping others and being positive about each other

Lesson 4	Lesson 5	Lesson 6
Callisthenics with unihoc sticks	Jog, freeze, change 'Listen to teacher'	Leaders take team warm-ups
All with unihoc sticks *Individual* Dribble Wall pass Stop *Pass* Pairs, control (reciprocal)	Re-cap all skills	*Skills circuit* Catching, passing, dribbling – hands Control, passing, dribbling – feet Control, pass, dribbling – sticks
4's Pass/control game	Organise teams for next week Allocate roles	
Pairs Reciprocal *Team* Coach control Careful with passes Stickers	Identify cooperative behaviours Stickers	Sum up Record results Improvement by all? Award certificates
	Cross-curricular teaching strategy Teacher talk, reinforcement Stickers chart and certificates Reciprocal teaching	

> I want to use 'modelling', as a strategy; the activity is football; what characteristic(s) can I hope to promote?
>
> Which teaching strategy could best achieve attitude improvement while teaching swimming?
>
> When using a reward system what activity would best achieve some independent action?

FIGURE 1.4   Questions to ask yourself during the planning

the left-hand side of the unit are the component parts of each lesson; 'introduction', 'development' or main body of lesson, and 'conclusion'. The additional item of 'cross-curricular element' is where the planner indicates how the teaching strategy will be implemented. At the bottom of the plan are details of the resources needed, how the unit will be assessed and what teaching strategy will be used to promote the affective (cross-curricular element).

This unit of work shows how *cooperation* will be targeted for six weeks, particularly emphasising helping others and being positive about one another. Each lesson begins with a brief discussion of the trait, or description of the reward system, or reinforcement of what is expected. In most lessons, you can structure the warm-up in such a way as to make use of cooperative behaviour. The development of each lesson includes a teacher strategy to point out something about cooperation and make the pupils realise why it is important and how it can be used. Finally, the conclusion usually has some teacher talk that restates or summarises the lesson. Here you would praise good cooperation and hand out the rewards, in this case the coloured stickers for the various encouraged behaviours and characteristics. Teacher talk and a reward system are the strategies used by this teacher. It can be seen that the teacher also makes use of reciprocal teaching. This is used fairly sparingly as this group is a Year 4 group. Because of their age they would have a limited knowledge base of the activities and reciprocal teaching in this instance would mean that pupils were relaying teacher's instructions to their partners, more than teaching themselves. The benefit is that there is some opportunity to work collaboratively on common ground.

This unit has all the necessary information that is required for you to plan in more detail the delivery of individual lessons.

Lesson Plans

Grineski (1993) suggests that physical education lessons should be led by instructional goal structures. He classifies these as competitive, individual and cooperative. Where goals are competitive, pupils work in opposition to achieve a goal that can only possibly be achieved by a few. Team matches, elimination games and knock-out tournaments would be examples of how this goal may be interpreted. Individual goals allow pupils to work alone to reach their goals. Examples of activities that could emphasise individual goals might be gymnastics, HRE and swimming. Cooperative instructional goals allow pupils to work together to try to achieve common goals. Grineski reports that there are 'higher levels of achievement, more favorable attitudes toward school, and higher levels of positive social interaction when learning was cooperatively structured rather than individualistically and competitively structured' (1993: 33).

It seems clear that matching instructional goals to what is expected from pupils in terms of achievement is a prerequisite to aiding development in pupils. If the purpose of a lesson is to encourage pupils to experience competition in a safe and protected environment, then a cooperative goal structure is probably not the best way to achieve that. Such a lesson might use a competitive goal structure, but mechanisms should be in place that allow children to continue to participate at a level appropriate to them rather than continue to have any limitations exposed to the whole class, as is the case with many elimination-type class structures. Even so, it would be better if all participants had an equal chance of winning.

A lesson planned around cooperative goal structures would be ideal for encouraging teamwork and possibly problem solving. This is more likely to maintain and promote positive social interactions with others. Trust, consideration of the contribution of others and feelings of personal worth are also likely to arise in this situation.

Individual goal structures may be usefully employed to help personal expression, the setting of individual goals and the perseverance to achieve those goals. Fitness regimes, personal improvement and skill mastery could be examples of the use of individual goal structures. The ability to adopt task orientation as opposed to ego orientation, as a measure of success, is crucial. Measurement against others when using individual goal structures would consign many pupils to feelings of failure. Teachers can help significantly with setting clear targets for individual pupils.

At a very basic level, one of the questions that you should ask of yourself is, 'What do I want the children to get from this lesson?' The answer to this question will determine not only the goal structure but also the type of activity that is employed in the lesson. The lesson plan in Table 1.2 is an example of how some of these guidelines can be put into practice.

Table 1.2 Lesson plan

Area of activity: Games	Key stage: 3
Unit title: Volleyball	Length of lesson: 40 mins
Class: 7y Number: 24	Lesson: 3 of 6

Objectives: *Psychomotor*: To refine and adapt the dig pass. To use the pass in a game. To analyse others' work and use the information to improve quality.
Affective: To work cooperatively in a group. To help each other. To work together towards group success.

Time	Activity	Organisation/equipment
10 mins	*Warm-up*	Individually

10 mins	*Skill development*	Demo: 'Sit where you can see and watch'
		  1. Show skill position
		  2. Demo: self-feed
		  3. Demo: partner-feed Q & A
		
		Drills for 3's (friendship groups)
		
		x_2 1. Feed and retrieve
		x_1 x_3 2. Perform
		  3. Coach
		
		gp gp gp gp
		gp gp gp gp
		
		'Keep up' in 3's

8 mins	*Conditioned game*	3 v. 3: same court One coach per team (rotate)
10 mins	*Concluding game*	3 games of 4 v. 4 Choose similar ability groups Lower net for less able players' games
2 mins	*Conclusion*	Sit and listen Q & A

Year: 7	
Equipment: 8 volley balls 4 badminton nets (net at 7 ft)	

Teaching points/differentiation	*Cross-curricular elements*
Jogging – 'freeze, change, up, down' Stretches – work down body. Volunteers demo	Lead with confidence
Wide strong legs – base Hands position Lock shoulders, straight arm platform Play shot from legs Monitor coaches for feedback – assist Assist coaches with less able 'Help each other with easy passes' Take turns to coach each other. Count passes Remember key points	Listen Respect other's space Pay attention Helping Reciprocal teaching Working together to improve quality one counts one coaches
Count passes Count shots over net Which game gets longest rally? Try to improve shots with each rally?	Being responsible – truthful in counting coaching–leadership
Use volley pass and dig/bump Each player must play ball before over Two players must play ball before over	Team membership Help each other
Restate teaching points Comment on affective programme	Cooperation Help Group success

As with the unit plan, there are administrative details at the top. The most pertinent of these are the objectives, both psychomotor and affective. This format shows the time for each activity, what that activity is, how it will be organised, teaching points, how the lesson will be differentiated for differing abilities and how the cross-curricular element will be catered for. Most teachers will recognise this as a fairly typical lesson plan. Where this one differs in a major way is that the teacher has also made provision for an area of affective development.

The pattern of the lesson will be familiar to teachers; warm-up followed by skill practice, then a conditioned game and a concluding activity or game. Following through each of the activities, it can be seen that the teacher has thought about the psychomotor outcomes and designed drills, practices and games to encourage that type of development. The affective objective is to work cooperatively in a group, to help each other and to work together towards group success. In each of the lesson components the teacher has outlined how this can be done.

During the warm-up, pupils are asked to volunteer to lead the stretching exercise, thereby encouraging them to show confidence in their ability to lead a group. While the teacher demonstrates the skill, pupils are asked to listen and respect each other's space while sitting and paying attention. The main body of the lesson, skill development activities, conditioned and concluding games, contain the main contribution to the achievement of the objectives. While working in threes, pupils are assigned different roles: one performs the skill, one feeds and retrieves and the third coaches the performer. They rotate these roles at the teacher's command. This method of reciprocal teaching needs some preparation, so the pupils will have been prepared by the question-and-answer session that determines their understanding of the task and the key coaching points to be observed. As the lesson progresses from skill development to conditioned game, the pupils are encouraged to be careful with their passes to each other; this helps their fellow group members perform the skill. The pupil coaching role is maintained throughout, devolving responsibility from the teacher to the pupils and allowing, and encouraging, them to help each other, and enabling each group to develop a degree of self-sufficiency. The concluding game reintroduces previously taught skills, the dig pass, and also imposes a competitive element. Two teams are joined together in a game, and each game seeks to achieve the criteria set by the teacher. The more able players are required to pass the ball to each team member before the ball goes over the net. Less able players are only asked to make two passes before the ball goes over the net. This type of differentiation is important because it provides all abilities with similar chances of success. The games are now scored so that the skills learned are put into a competitive situation. There is no comparison between games, although there will be winning and losing teams. Scorers and coaches are appointed to each game by the teacher and the theme of cooperation and helping each other within the team towards team success is continued.

You will notice straightaway that, although the affective objective is cooperation, there is a competitive element. This is a recognition that competition is an essential component of most sporting activities. It is introduced in this lesson as an example of the way in which cooperative play can help a team to achieve group, competitive success. Other lessons and units could be designed which eliminate the experience of competition. This is an equally legitimate objective in physical education. You will also notice that the inclusion of an affective dimension in the planning and implementation of the lesson has not detracted from the physical dimension of the subject. Most teachers could comfortably achieve the delivery of such a lesson. The added bonus is an additional emphasis, not added work!

Context

These suggested methods of constructing units of work and lesson plans provide useful structural frameworks that can be used for a number of purposes. Using the suggestions made earlier, it is fairly easy for student teachers and teachers to see and experience the relevance of the material they are using. Teachers planning their units and lessons in this way are actively engaging in the concept of this new approach; they are taking 'ownership' of their work by becoming intimately involved in its construction.

This has importance for application with children in schools. If we apply the concept of context to a school situation, we can see that it is linked to the notion of active learning. Physical skills are taught by providing the pupils with the opportunities to practise those skills. We do not teach the side foot pass in soccer only by telling the pupils how to do it. We set up practices and game situations that facilitate optimum learning opportunities. We allow the pupils to *do* the skill. Thus, the pupils are active in their learning. The same approach is necessary with affective elements of physical education. In the examples used here, the pupils have opportunities to engage in cooperative behaviours in a variety of ways. Similarly, to encourage sportsmanship it is best to engage the pupils in sportsmanship scenarios and decision making. Merely stating that we, the teachers, want them to show cooperation or sportsmanship is not enough on its own. Obviously, some element of teacher talk will be required, but pupils must then be allowed to practise the skill, for example cooperation or sportsmanship, in relevant situations. They must be allowed to practise in a practical, relevant and contextual way.

A CASE STUDY

The case study used here to illustrate the planning phase of this new approach reports the project of a final year Bachelor of Education student (Rowe, 1995). A number of students had attended a series of workshops aimed at helping them to include social and personal objectives in their teaching of physical education at the primary level and Jane's (pseudonym) work arose out of that.

The task was to plan, implement and assess the effectiveness of a six-week unit of work for gymnastics. It was Jane's intention to place the appropriate affective objectives alongside the psychomotor objectives for maximum effect.

TABLE 1.3   Jane's unit of work

Area of activity: Gymnastic activities		*Unit title*: Gym: weight transfer	
Key stage: 1		*Year*: 2	
Lesson structure	*Lesson 1*	*Lesson 2*	*Lesson 3*
Introduction	Different ways of travel – feet	Move on feet in different directions	Travel alternating feet and hands on floor
Development Floor	Rocking on body parts Link movements	Standing, curl, uncurl Hands on floor – Kick feet same place Kick feet different place	Rolling on floor, come to stand Run, jump, land on feet – weight on hands or weight on feet
Apparatus	Onto apparatus – hold 3 secs – off apparatus	Add control	Travel on apparatus on hands and feet. Stop on other body part
Conclusion	Hands on floor, kick feet in air	Take weight on hands longer	Practise run, jump sequence
Cross-curricular element	Intro SPA Pre-test 1st group selected Certificates	SPA Praise effort as well as ability Certificates	SPA Ask pupils to praise good work Teacher encouragement Certificates
Resources needed Mats, boxes, benches, beams		*Assessment criteria* Physical element by teacher observation Affective element by self-esteem scale	

During the workshops, she had been impressed by the teaching strategies suggested in the work of McHugh (1995). Although it was Jane's idea to attempt to develop self-esteem in her pupils, she was acutely aware that it was not adequate to adopt just any teaching strategy, but to use those most suited to the psychomotor *and* affective objectives.

To make the planning process easier, Jane decided to do a separate unit plan for the affective objectives and then incorporate this into a regular unit plan at a later stage. The final unit plan can be seen in Table 1.3. For an experienced teacher this would be tedious, but for a student teacher it enabled her to differentiate the varying objectives.

Time (lessons × mins): 6 × 40 mins

Objectives   *Prac* – Plan and perform simple linked actions. Practise and improve performance
               Aff – To improve self-esteem through praise and SPA

Lesson 4	*Lesson 5*	*Lesson 6*
Feet to hands changing direction	Feet to hands Smooth links	Practise feet – hands travel sequence
Support, roll, support Different parts Practise last week's sequence – links Refine last week's sequences	Jump, land, curl, roll, stand Run, jump, land, hands, feet, shapes in air Continue last week's work	Make up sequence using learnt movements Experiment, practise, refine new sequences
Refine sequence	Practise best sequence	Free practice of previous work
SPA Pupils praise effort Certificates	SPA Teacher restate idea Certificates	SPA Certificates Post-test

Cross-curricular teaching strategy
Smiley People Award (SPA)
Teacher praise and encouragement

The strategy that Jane used was a reward system called the Smiley People Award (SPA). This was supported by teacher praise and encouragement during the lessons. The SPA is an acknowledgement of a person's special worth as a person. It is not awarded for physical ability, but spread around the group so that during the course of the unit of work, each pupil receives the award at least once. A group of five or six children were chosen for special recognition at the beginning of each lesson. The pupils were chosen alphabetically and were different each week. They came to the front of the class and the teacher awarded each of them a coloured band for easy recognition throughout the lesson. It was hoped that the pupils working alongside the Smiley People would pay them special attention, in addition to that given by the teacher. At the end of the lesson the Smiley People were again called to the front of the class and exchanged their coloured band for an SPA, a badge with their name on it.

It can be seen from the unit of work plan that the gymnastic activities that Jane employed are non-competitive. The children do not have to show their work to others, only to the teacher. This eliminates any possibility of too much ego orientation and aids in the adoption of task orientation. This means that the children are not concerned with how they perform in relation to others, merely how they perform in relation to the required tasks in the lesson. The teacher begins by introducing the idea of the SPA and links this to early praise for behaviour and effort. Later in the unit, the demonstration of physical competence is also praised. Children are asked to comment on each other's effort and good work. The whole atmosphere is one of learning together, being supportive and non-judgemental, and taking pleasure in the achievements of all in the class.

Jane decided to assess her pupils' self-esteem development by using an adaptation of Rosenberg's Global Self-Esteem Scale (Figure 1.5). This is a short (ten-item) Likert scale instrument using a pre- and post-test method. She had piloted the scale with a primary school class beforehand and had changed a few of the items as a result of feedback from the children, the teacher and her tutor. It was mostly the language that had to be changed to allow the children to understand what they were being asked.

Items 2, 5, 6, 8 and 9 are scored sa $= 1$, a $= 2$, d $= 3$ and sd $= 4$. Items 1, 3, 4, 7 and 10 are scored sa $= 4$, a $= 3$, d $= 2$ and sd $= 1$. Jane used the pre-test and post-test scores to assess whether the children's individual self-esteem had improved or not. Jane's adaptation of the scale was not validated in the scientific sense, and she did recognise this in her report. However, when used together with her observations of the class and each individual's behaviour, the results did give an idea of the trend in self-esteem development.

Jane found that over two-thirds of her class had improved their self-esteem scores during the course of the unit of work. The maximum score was 40 and the average improvement in self-esteem score was nearly 7 points, quite a large

Please circle the answer that best describes how YOU feel				
	strongly agree	agree	disagree	strongly disagree
1. I think I'm OK.	sa	a	d	sd
2. Sometimes I think I'm no good.	sa	a	d	sd
3. Some things about me are good.	sa	a	d	sd
4. I can do things as well as anyone.	sa	a	d	sd
5. I don't have much to be proud of.	sa	a	d	sd
6. Sometimes I feel useless.	sa	a	d	sd
7. I'm as good as anyone else.	sa	a	d	sd
8. I wish I could like myself more.	sa	a	d	sd
9. I feel like a failure.	sa	a	d	sd
10. I feel good about myself.	sa	a	d	sd

FIGURE 1.5   Global Self-Esteem Scale (adapted)

gain. She had a control group, a class that she taught in the normal way, and their scores stayed roughly the same.

However, the point of this example is not really the results, although they are fairly impressive. The point is that the planning that is needed when incorporating affective objectives and teaching strategies into units of work can quite easily be done. Values and objectives need to be considered, strategies selected, and activities modified to reflect the different emphasis. It requires a little extra consideration and thought, but the rewards are clearly worth it.

THE THEORY

Effective Teaching

Much research has been conducted into what an effective teacher is, what makes an effective teacher and what behaviours and characteristics an effective teacher exhibits. Although this is not the place for a comprehensive account of that research, it is worth identifying a few of the key findings about effective teaching:

■ knowledge of subject
■ planning and preparation
■ management and organisation
■ communication
■ provide learning environment
■ hold pupils accountable
■ understand social process
■ provide feedback and time on task.

At the forefront of these findings is the fact that teachers must have a good knowledge of their subject. This would seem to go without saying, but lack of confidence in subject knowledge is something that many student teachers complain about. Usually these fears are unfounded, and mastery of content emerges as a strength by the end of a teacher's education. As with many things in life, being prepared is the key to success. The relevant chapters in this book will certainly help teachers with their planning and preparation, particularly when teaching within this different approach. Being able to manage a class of pupils and organise them effectively is also a good way to reduce any discipline problems that might otherwise emerge. An ability to communicate effectively not only allows instructions to be understood and carried out, but also promotes positive relationships with pupils. Many schoolchildren say that they relate well to their physical education teacher, and communication skills and approachability are the reason for this. Perhaps the most important factor is the teachers' ability to provide a learning environment for their pupils. This means that they provide appropriate tasks and practices, at the right level of difficulty, and at the right time. The atmosphere must be supportive, positive, safe (emotionally as well as physically) and enjoyable. Having said that, the most effective teachers also hold their pupils accountable for their actions in class. These teachers keep a careful check on pupils' progress and help pupils to be responsible for their own learning and participation. Sometimes pupils and teachers come to the same class with differing agendas. Teachers have an instructional agenda, but pupils also have a social agenda; they want to have a good time and enjoy their physical education lessons. If teachers understand this, they can accommodate both sets of requirements in their planning, to the detriment of neither. Lastly, there is the technical necessity that teachers provide accurate and timely feedback and ensure that pupils spend enough time on tasks to improve their skills, or in the case of the affective domain, their personal and social characteristics.

These characteristics are borne out by the research. When comparing the characteristics of teachers categorised as most and least effective, Phillips and Carlisle (1983) found that the teacher's ability to analyse pupil needs was a significant contribution to pupil achievement. This ability incorporated knowledge of content, use of objectives and flexibility and appropriateness of instruction. They also found that the best way to increase skill learning was to maximise pupil practice time while achieving a reasonably high level of success. Phillips and Carlisle's work, and most of the teacher effectiveness research, have focused on physical skill acquisition. These teacher behaviours provide a bedrock for what constitutes a 'good teacher'. The proposition in the new approach towards an eclectic, philanthropic pedagogy is to maintain this good practice while at the same time developing awareness and further teaching skills, thus developing a more complete teacher who can facilitate a child's holistic development.

Teaching Styles and Strategies

There is often confusion between teaching style and teaching strategy. Teaching style refers to an overall paradigm, or set of teacher behaviours that combine to produce a recognisable type of teacher. So a teacher who is clearly 'in charge', who directs the lesson completely, chooses groups, sets tasks and time limits, is a teacher in the command style; a didactic teacher. A teacher who allows pupils to work in friendship groups, allows pupils to set tasks within given parameters and encourages pupils to give feedback to their partners is a more pupil-centred-style teacher. Mosston and Ashworth (1990) provide a more formalised concept of teaching styles. They characterise teaching styles on a continuum, or 'spectrum', from a command style at one end to a discovery style at the other. These styles have varying degrees of teacher and pupil input and are more, or less, teacher-centred or pupil-centred depending on their position on the continuum.

A teaching strategy refers to a specific teaching behaviour, or action, or tactic. A teacher selects strategies to achieve certain educational objectives within lessons. For example, a teacher might make frequent use of a question-and-answer technique to ensure that pupils are learning the information presented; or a teacher might use small-sided, conditioned games to practise certain skills and check whether they have been mastered enough to use them in game situations. These are teaching strategies, designed to highlight a particular aspect of learning within the lesson. Taken together, a group of strategies selected by the teacher can be representative of a teaching style. Several teaching strategies that are particularly suitable for developing personal and social characteristics are described later in 'The Practice' section.

Learning Theories

A most pertinent question is, 'How will children learn these things?' Theories of learning tend to fit into two categories, the social-learning theory and the structural-development theory. The learning of personal and social skills and the development of attitudes and values, as well as the learning of physical skills, are partially explained by these theories. Social learning is based on observing behaviours of others and adopting and demonstrating those behaviours. Children copy and mimic actions of significant others; these are usually their friends, parents and teachers. Therefore, a teacher who models a certain behaviour is a powerful learning agent for a number of children who will copy that behaviour. They value what the teacher does and says and therefore they try to act like him or her.

Structural-development learning claims that children behave in a certain way because of the reactions of others and the environment. Classroom interaction and peer pressure are great determinants of some pupils' behaviour. To change one's behaviour as a result of the actions and reactions of others locates that learning firmly in the structural-development arena.

It is entirely possible that children learn some behaviours in a social-learning way and other behaviours through a structural-development mode. A teacher must therefore provide a variety of opportunities for the children in their classes to learn in a variety of ways. Modelling socially desirable behaviours is important, but so is giving pupils chances to react with each other in social situations. In their most simplistic forms, social-learning theory lends itself to being teacher-determined and -led, and structural-development theory is more likely to be learner-centred and -led. This oversimplifies a complex process, but the knowledge of this process does provide additional strategies for teachers to use in promoting the personal and social development of their pupils.

Learning Styles

Although learning is related to these theoretical models, it is also affected by the learning style of the participants. In general terms, the older the pupils, the higher their conceptual complexity level (or their ability to understand). So low-conceptual-complexity pupils, or younger pupils, are more comfortable with more didactic, structured approaches. Pupils with higher conceptual levels can more readily take advantage of learner-centred methods. Teachers should not necessarily expect younger pupils to discover for themselves the best ways of performing skills; it is more likely that they will need to be shown how to do it. In these cases, demonstrating is a vital teaching skill. By the same token, older pupils with high conceptual complexity levels will probably be able to solve problems and apply previously learnt skills in new contexts. This can also be applied to social and personal characteristics. In a simple form, children of high conceptual complexity levels may be able to respond to verbal information such as teacher talk, whereas children of lower conceptual complexity levels would probably benefit more from the teacher modelling the required traits as well.

When learning skills and behaviours, children search for cues that help in that learning process. Older children find it easier to focus on relevant cues. Younger children scan all cues before identifying which ones are relevant. Reducing information given to young pupils to crucial components, and restricting extraneous variables, can enable them to more quickly identify the cues that will help their learning.

Much of this is merely good teaching practice and teachers will be familiar with many of the concepts. It is important to realise that changing, or influencing, social and personal characteristics is only an extension of skill learning and as such, many of the same principles apply. (For those interested in reading more of this theoretical perspective, see Lee, 1993; Mawer, 1995; and Siedentop, 1991.)

THE PRACTICE

Because different teaching strategies are selected to promote specific educational objectives within lessons, it is essential to have a knowledge of what it is that certain strategies can be expected to achieve. This will allow you to select the most appropriate strategies for your needs. The following strategies are designed to promote aspects of personal, social and moral development, commonly known as the affective domain of physical education. What follows is not a global catalogue of all the activities that you can employ; rather it suggests a few tried and tested ideas that will give you a starting point for developing your own strategies. Personally developed strategies will have more relevance, and be far more context-specific, than those gleaned from other people's writings. The thinking and planning process necessary to create strategies gives you more control and 'ownership' of your lessons and therefore more personal involvement.

General Programme Advice

When teachers and pupils are involved in a new venture, as in these cases, there need to be some guidelines that both teachers and pupils are aware of and are expected to follow. Compagnone (1995) suggests some of the following considerations from his experience of working with responsibility programmes.

Start the programme at the beginning of a term. It is obviously easier for pupils and teachers to start when rules and routines are being established with a new class. The start of a new school year is a most appropriate place to begin.

Build in time for reflection. This is important for the teachers as well as for the pupils. Even though teachers will have planned the intervention and will know where they are going, it is worthwhile having the opportunity to subjectively evaluate 'how it's going' at periods during the term or year. Similarly for the pupils, getting their perspective and feedback helps with future planning and implementation.

Pupil involvement is crucial. Programmes of this nature will only work if the subjects, that is the pupils, are involved and committed to the outcomes. This is why the use of reflection/feedback times and teaching strategies such as reciprocal teaching are important. Explain what you are trying to do and achieve. If there is time, discuss how it will work, how it will differ from normal lessons, how they will be assessed (if at all), what your expectations are. Explain what you are trying to do and achieve. With some constructive guidance, it is entirely possible that their view will coincide with yours! This means that you and the class will be working towards a common goal.

Be persistent. These behaviour modification strategies can take a long time to work, so do not be disappointed by slow progress. The research is quite clear that prosocial behaviours, such as responsibility, can be positively effected. Remember that this will be new to the children, just as it is probably new to you. When learning any new skill, some people master it straightaway, others take longer. It will be the same with social and personal skills. There will be problems and failures, but these will provide opportunities for problem-solving and progress.

School-wide emphasis. Any programme of this type will be more successful if it is pursued on a school-wide basis. This has been shown with health education and health-related exercise. The revised National Curriculum (QCA, 1999b) and the proposed framework for PSHE (QCA, 1999a) provide a rationale and justification for such a school-wide approach. Physical education is uniquely placed to be at the forefront of these developments and will thus benefit from these political initiatives.

Embarrassment and falseness. Your efforts and the responses of the children may, at first, seem false and there could be some embarrassment at behaving in a way with which class members are unfamiliar. This self-conscious and unnatural feeling will wear off and the prosocial behaviours will become natural. Research has shown this to be the case. This takes time, so be patient, persevere and be tolerant of failures. Think back to the first time that you stood in front of a class; those nerves wore off eventually and so will these initial feelings of discomfort.

Cooperative Behaviours

Cooperative Games

Simply put, cooperative games reward working together, whereas competitive games reward working against each other, or against the other team.

Keep the rally going. An example of this cooperative game would be a tennis or volleyball game where the objective is to keep a rally going for as long as possible, whereas in most tennis or volleyball games one side tries to beat another by ending the rally. This is ideally suited to stroke practice, in tennis for example. One player practises forehand ground strokes and her partner on the other side of the net practises his backhand ground strokes. There can be winners if required; the *game*, or the *group*, or the *pair* that has the most rallies is the most successful. Teams, or pairs, involved in this type of game could also try to beat their previous 'best rally score', thus eliminating any competition

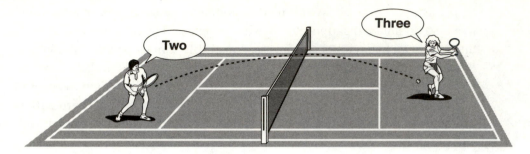

FIGURE 2.1   Tennis rally

with other groups. There is one obvious problem with this type of game: it places no value on the winning shot or on aggressive play. The danger here is that this detracts from the essential competitive characteristics of these sports. It should be remembered, however, that we are advocating the teaching of cooperation, and other prosocial behaviours, but not to the exclusion of all else. Cooperative games can therefore be incorporated into lesson plans when necessary.

Conditioned games. Teachers commonly adapt game rules to accommodate differing abilities within classes. This strategy can be applied here. For example, each team member must touch the ball before a score can be made; or the passes must be boy – girl – boy – girl and so on; players change positions so that all pupils get a chance to play in all the positions. It will be apparent that these strategies would be unwieldy with most full team games; passing to each member of a team in an 11-a-side football game would require a level of skill not possessed by many professional teams! This encourages teachers to employ the good educational practice of using small-sided, conditioned games. Thus, in a three versus three basketball game it is easier to apply the condition that each player must receive and pass the ball before a shot can be made (Figure 2.2). This is one strategy in which it might be better to impose sanctions against antisocial behaviour. The deduction of a point for swearing or the awarding of a penalty against the team for arguing can be used to good effect. The problem with rewarding prosocial behaviours in game situations is that the players could concentrate more on that than the game. You could end up with a situation in which players are more concerned with passing compliments than passing the ball or competing in the game!

Reciprocal and Small Group Teaching

These teaching arrangements ensure that pupils must work together to produce effective outcomes. It is your responsibility to ensure that the task is clearly set and that pupils understand their roles. You should demonstrate, or model, the

FIGURE 2.2   Basketball passing

task and make sure that the pupils are held accountable for their work. Having spent time early in the lesson establishing the way the lesson will work, you can then closely monitor, guide and intervene in pair or group work throughout the remainder of the lesson.

As an example, groups of three could be engaged in a free throw shooting practice in basketball (not illustrated). You demonstrate the skill two or three times, describing clearly the key teaching points such as, 'uncoil the legs and body, ball hand on top of the head, extend the arm and "break" the wrist at the end of the shot, nice high arc'. Dividing the class into groups of three, you can then assign roles; one is the shooter, another is the coach, and the third one is the retriever/scorer. As the class practises you should move around the groups checking on the progress and augmenting the feedback from the 'coach'.

The roles are rotated so that all the children play all the parts. In this way, the pupils are practising a skill, they are learning to work in small groups, they are developing cognitive and social skills and they are learning to accept constructive criticism and help from their peers. You have set the task and the attendant parameters, you have ensured that the practice has taken place effectively and you have devolved some responsibility to individual pupils that hopefully encourages them to practise cooperatively.

FIGURE 2.3   Reciprocal teaching

Using Children's Ideas

When first introducing the idea of cooperative learning to children, it is important to explain to them the concept and clarify any issues arising. Just as teachers must believe in what they are attempting, it is best if children can be persuaded of the importance and benefits of a cooperative approach. While teachers will have their own ideas about what are the important concepts to be promoted, the pupils may well share some of these concepts and also put forward some others.

You can begin by explaining what the programme is and how it will develop for the rest of the term. This could be followed by asking the pupils what they think are the important points about 'working together'. This is probably best done in a subsequent lesson when the pupils have had a chance to experience the programme.

These pupil ideas can be listed on the blackboard, or on a flip chart (Underwood and Williams, 1991). You can then tidy up and collate the responses into a chart that can be displayed in each lesson. You can use such a visual aid in a number of ways. First, you could use the chart to point out these important cooperative factors at the beginning of each lesson and perhaps suggest which ones are appropriate for the day's lesson. Secondly, during the lesson, you could illustrate any incidences of cooperative behaviour that occur by pointing them out on the chart. Thirdly, the chart could serve as a focal point

FIGURE 2.4   Teacher putting children's ideas on chart/board

which enables you to instigate a class discussion on progress. You might want to lead with questions such as, 'Which of these are you doing best?', 'Are there any other things that we ought to add up here?', 'Which ones do we need to work on most?'and 'How can we improve on these things?'

Sportsmanship and Fair Play

All sports, games and physical activities include something of the notion of morality. This is usually manifested in playing fairly and doing the right thing. It is very difficult for sports and games to operate without sportsmanship and moral behaviour playing a crucial part. This is especially true at school, recreation and amateur level. It would seem therefore that school physical education is an ideal vehicle for promoting ideas of playing fair and being a good sport.

Morality does not exist in isolation. It is based on a system of values. To a large degree, teachers work in an educational community that has, and imposes, a set of common values. These values are apparent when we see what is required, that is mandated, in the school curriculum. Thus, personal, social and health benefits are valued; an idea of religious beliefs, tolerance and spirituality is valued; equity of provision is valued; as are the core and foundation subjects and the cross-curricular themes. It is as well that there is an underpinning system of values; it would be impossible to construct a learning situation for each moral dilemma. In the following examples it is clear that there is an assumption that morality and fairness in all aspects of democratic society are values that are worth promoting.

Fair play points

This is relatively simple to operate. Pupils are awarded a point for each instance of sportsmanship or fair play that they demonstrate. This can be restricted to game play or it could be in all physical education activities. The teacher, or non-participating pupils, keep a record of points awarded and they are accumulated over the course of a term, or perhaps a whole year. Points can be awarded to individuals or to teams. In the 'Fair Play Points Chart' (Figure 2.5), points are being accumulated for the award of certificates and they also contribute towards a favourable comment in the pupils' school reports.

As long as there is some tangible evidence that pupils are being rewarded for appropriate behaviour, such as the instances suggested in this example, they will value their contribution to fair play points. If the strategy is used in game

Figure 2.5   Fair play points chart

play with set teams, fair play league tables could be kept and sporting teams could be rewarded in similar ways.

This particular strategy has been tested by Giebink and McKenzie (1985). They tested three strategies for improving sportsmanship in physical education: instruction and praise, modelling and a points system. All three strategies enhanced sportsmanlike behaviours, but a points system, with timely reinforcements from the teacher, was by far the most powerful of the three.

Fair Play Scenarios

This can work in discussion or in activity. Ideal scenarios are those that have appeared on TV the night or day before. With video-replay and expert analysis, we are continually being presented with controversial situations in many sports events. A five-minute discussion, even in the changing room, about an event broadcast on TV can be used to illustrate a number of points. 'Was it fair?', 'Was it within the rules?', 'What would you have done in that situation?'and 'Does that happen in school sport?' are all questions that will generate some discussion.

Practical fair play scenarios can easily be set up in lesson time. Getting players to referee their own games and appointing children as officials are two obvious ways in which the importance of fair play can be illustrated. There will inevitably be disagreements to begin with, but these can be profitably used to emphasise that for a game to take place effectively, the conventions of fair play must be observed. Disagreements will gradually decrease as the pupils get used to playing fairly and accepting the referee's decision, even when the referee is a classmate. Games could also be played without officials. Children can be encouraged to be honest about line calls and admit when they have committed fouls. As with the other scenarios, there will be disagreement at first, but this can be used as an opportunity to discuss the problem and encourage fair play as a way forward. Children do not want to argue all the time and they will quickly realise that the spirit of the game needs to be adhered to if they are to be able to play without too much disruption.

Fair Play Games

A most simple and effective game is any situation that requires self-scoring and self-report. Children have an acute sense of fair play; that is what allows them to play their games without adult supervision. There is a feeling that they must be true to themselves and to each other. There will be those children who have more forceful personalities and they will tend to lead and possibly dominate the games; but by the same token there will be those who are happy to be led, or just 'go along with the others', so that they may take part in game play. This

FIGURE 2.6   Passing a soccer ball

interaction and negotiation eventually reach a consensus that allows a game to take place. In this way an organic and flexible status quo is reached.

An example of this would be pairs passing a soccer ball between two cones (Figure 2.6). Each pair has to keep count of the number of successful passes. When the pairs report their number of passes at the end of the practice, it will be apparent to you, and particularly to the children, if any pair has been dishonest. With the benefit of some later discussion and teacher talk, dishonesty in presenting results will quickly disappear. The most powerful sanction is that of peer disapproval and pressure to conform to the norms of sportsmanlike and fair behaviour.

'Fair Play for Kids'

Fair Play for Kids is basically a teacher resource manual produced by the Commission for Fair Play (1990) in Canada. The programme includes teaching strategies based on both the social-learning and the structural-development theories of learning. The first two described below are located in social-learning theory.

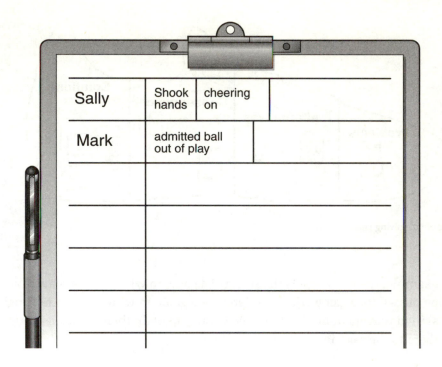

Sally	Shook hands	cheering on	
Mark	admitted ball out of play		

FIGURE 2.7   Compliment chart

Compliment chart. Pupils in the class keep their own notes as a record of fair play by others. (It might be more effective to have non-participating pupils keeping the notes.) These are collated by the teacher and the pupils who have done particularly well, or improved significantly, are recognised at the end of each week.

Fair play agreement. Pupils are asked to list some behaviours that demonstrate fair play. During the lesson, pupils must attempt to use those fair play behaviours. At the close of the lesson, pupils can reflect individually on whether they have achieved their fair play behaviour target. As pupils get used to this, teachers might like to introduce some element of sharing each other's experiences with the group, time permitting.

The following two strategies from the *Fair Play for Kids* programme are located in structural development theory:

Invent a game. Small groups of pupils are set the task of inventing games, or rules for games, to overcome certain unfair situations set by the teacher. For

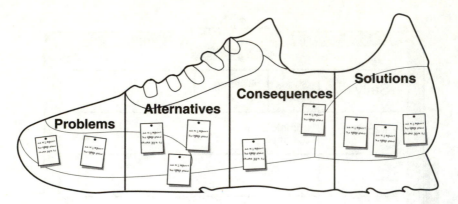

FIGURE 2.8   Problem-solving running shoe

example, the teacher sets the scene of a game in which some players are not to be passed to; a game with no referee; or a game in which only a few highly skilled players dominate the play. Groups explain their solutions and teach them to the remaining class.

Problem-solving running shoe. The primary school years would be the best location for using this strategy. It is designed to help resolve conflicts. It employs a large poster of a running shoe subdivided into areas labelled *problems*, *alternatives*, *consequences* and *solutions*.

Pupils in conflicts are directed to the running shoe to complete the areas and solve the conflict. A less time-consuming alternative would be for you to take one or two dilemmas each week and have the whole class work on them together.

Individual Traits

Emotional Safety

Children need to feel safe in school. As physical educators, we are critically aware of children's physical safety. Lessons are planned with safety in mind; gymnasia, sports halls, playing fields and equipment are designed, built and then checked before each lesson with safety in mind; and practices and games are supervised with safety in mind. In general, children are physically safe in schools and in physical education lessons. However, emotional safety is a different thing. Physical education is very much a 'public' subject. Performances are on display for all to see. One cannot hide one's physical efforts in an exercise book.

In addition to the 'public display' aspect of the subject, other factors can influence children's feelings of emotional safety and security. Whether we like it or not, many of the activities that constitute physical education have gender connotations attached to them. In its simplest sense, many children perceive netball, dance and gymnastics as feminine, and football, rugby and cricket as masculine. Teachers need to be aware of these perceptions and to work hard to overcome them from the earliest opportunity. To expose children to 'emotionally unsafe' situations, especially from a gender point of view, opens them up to ridicule from their peers. The use of gender-neutral language and the invocation of positive role models can be useful. If boys can see, perhaps on a video, just how difficult some gymnastic movements are, and how strong participants have to be to perform those movements, then they are more likely to respect participation in that activity. Similarly, if girls can be shown the high skill level of women football and rugby players, it is possible that they might aspire to emulate role models from those sports.

To develop their self-esteem, and also their physical skills, children need to feel secure. They need to be able to try without fear of ridicule. In short, they must be emotionally safe. Rather than set games or strategies for promoting emotional safety, Helion (1996) gives us some guidelines to be considered.

People should not be hurt. People should not come into contact with physical harm or psychological harm. Actions, words and attitudes that harm others should not be tolerated in an educational environment.

There is no place for sarcasm in education. Following on from the previous item, sarcasm is negative and harmful and children who suffer sarcasm certainly do not learn anything beneficial from the experience. They merely learn that they are failures and therefore worthy of ridicule.

There is no such thing as a stupid question. Questions are indicators that further information is required or that an interest has been aroused, and as such should be welcomed by the teacher. However, some children do not hear because they do not listen to instructions in the first place. This should lead us to question why they were not listening; did the teacher establish a quiet class before explaining, did the teacher explain clearly, did she or he check that everyone understood before beginning the activity? If pupils are discouraged from asking questions, then it is possible that a quest for knowledge and information could expire – the last thing an educator wants.

Physical education is for everyone. It may be the case in organised sports that an élite is rewarded by winning. But physical education is not just for that élite, it is for all children. To place too much emphasis on winning and losing and not enough on participating, learning and enjoying is to teach that physical education, and later physical activity, is only for the gifted few. Much has been written about inclusive physical education for those with physical disabilities; this could just as easily apply to those with different levels of ability. Paradoxically, this inclusion for those with physical disabilities *can* be seen at an élite level in the Special Olympics in the USA and internationally in the Paralympics. Nevertheless, even though competitive sport can now be available to everyone, it is a responsibility of a school subject to make its subject matter, that is the sports and games and activities that constitute physical education, available to children of all ability levels.

Be a role model. It is not enough to tell children how to act and behave. We have an obligation to demonstrate the behaviours that we expect from children. If we talk about fair play, we must be fair in all our endeavours. If we tell children not to be sarcastic, we must not be sarcastic either. Teachers who, in class, say that winning is not everything, must demonstrate that ethos when their school team has lost a game.

Games are only games. Games are for enjoyment. For all their importance in the adult world, in the children's world they should be fun and enjoyable. Although it's nice to win, children should be taught that participation and enjoyment of the activity are far more important than any demonstration of physical supremacy. By definition, there can only be one winner, but winners need losers, and the game needs both. Children must learn that the game is worth playing for its own sake.

Self-esteem

Pupils enjoy being recognised by the teacher. However, we as teachers know that it is usually the good pupils and the not-so-good pupils who initially tend to command attention. It is easier, and natural, to notice the opposing ends of the spectrum, both in motor-ability terms and in behaviour terms. In spite of this tendency, teachers are generally good at learning and remembering children's names. It is the recognition of themselves as individuals that children value, not just the fact that their name is known. The two strategies that follow have been adapted from an American context (McHugh, 1995). They indicate to pupils that teachers value and recognise them as people, not just as schoolchildren, and they also indicate that it is not just physical abilities that can earn them praise and recognition in physical education lessons. This encourages self-esteem development and helps induce in the children a feeling of self-worth. It shows that their worth as people is not based purely on physical abilities.

Most Valuable Person (MVP). This is a derivative of the 'most valuable player'

FIGURE 2.9   Child receiving a Most Valuable Person (MVP) award

concept prevalent in American sport. The idea is based on the premise that one player has the most beneficial influence on the outcome of the game. As this would be contrary to the ethos of any programme to promote affective development, a number of adaptations are necessary.

Each class member in turn is recognised as the MVP for the day. This eliminates the élitism of the best player or the best-behaved always being selected for the award. The MVP could be allowed to lead the warm-up, choose team names, pick the concluding activity from a few suggested by the teacher, or be a team captain. This will encourage each individual to feel a little bit special, at least for one lesson; they will have the chance to demonstrate some leadership skills; and they will enjoy a raised status within their peer group.

The 'sunshine-gram'. In a non-USA context, this might be called 'notes home'. During the course of the term you send to each child's home a note which has a positive comment about that child (Figure 2.10). The note could be about anything positive that has happened in class or at school. The note could mention anything from effort in class, to helping others, to showing good skill.

Not only does this benefit individual children, it increases positive contact with parents, thus performing useful public relations for the subject and the school. This need not take up too much extra time. Computer-generated notes can be easily individualised with very little effort.

Catch the children being good. It is part of a teacher's job to limit poor behaviour. Because of this, we become quite good at catching bad behaviour

> Dear Mr & Mrs Jones,
>
> I just thought you'd like to know that David has been a great help in PE this week. He has worked very hard in helping others in the class.
>
> Yours sincerely
>
> Alan Smith
>
> (PE Teacher)

FIGURE 2.10   A 'sunshine-gram'

almost as soon as it starts. A novel twist would be to 'catch the children being good'. Identification of good actions and the associated praise let pupils know that you are serious about what you have said about behaviour. Most children love to be called by the teacher by name, especially when it is to comment in a positive manner.

Responsibility

It has already been shown that teaching physical education to enhance personal, social and environmental responsibility is a popular theme in the USA. Parker, Kallusky and Hellison (1999) suggest a few guidelines that teachers could adopt relatively easily without any disruption to their normal lesson planning or conduct of lessons.

Allow pupils to adjust tasks to match their needs. Aspects of the task that pupils may be allowed to change could be complexity of task, choice of equipment, choice of competition level. For example: pupils could be allowed to choose two-handed catching if one-handed was beyond them; bean bags might be easier to catch than cricket balls; and some pupils would appreciate the choice of a recreational game rather than a competitive game. Of course, there will be pupils who will want to test their skills with harder tasks and in competitive environments. These could also be accommodated.

Allow more peer involvement. Examples of this might be more reciprocal, or peer teaching, and some element of self-assessment or peer-assessment. Pupils can easily help each other with simple skills and can also assess whether they are being done correctly. In this case you would perform a very active monitoring and intervention role rather than a didactic, pedagogic role.

Encourage pupils into small community (school) projects. Helping to mend equipment, 'stock-taking' equipment, helping with clubs for younger pupils –

these are all possible with some encouragement. The encouragement need not be a reward as such, for it is important to stress the altruistic nature of these opportunities.

Developing responsibility in school pupils does not assume a lack of responsibility to begin with. Developing responsibility involves making pupils aware of different levels of being responsible (Hellison, 1985). Some children may need to become more individually responsible, others may be able to assume responsibility in a wider arena such as community involvement or team leadership. As an aid to increasing the level of their responsibility, pupils can become involved in goal-setting. This means self-evaluation of where they are now, proposing where they want to get to and devising ways of getting there.

TABLE 2.1   Am I responsible for myself?

	Yes	No	Sometimes
1 I can work well on my own			
2 If I get it wrong it's my fault			
3 I make sure my kit is ready for PE			
4 I can motivate myself			
5 I try hard to get better			

A simple self-report, such as the one above, will give pupils an indication of their level of self-responsibility. The more ticks in the 'yes' column, the more self-responsible the pupils are. A majority of ticks in the 'no' or 'sometimes' columns would indicate that the pupil does not have a very good level of self-responsibility. If we take the situation where a pupil needs to improve in this area, what can be done?

Begin by identifying where the child can make a difference. For example, they could begin to accept responsibility for their own PE kit, or try their hardest in each lesson. They can then construct a simple checklist to keep account of their progress in these areas.

We can see from Table 2.2 that this pupil is making progress in taking responsibility for getting his or her PE kit ready, but is not being so responsible for his or her own efforts in physical education lessons. On days when there are two ticks, this could be followed up with another teaching strategy such as simple recognition of effort or a complimentary note home at the end of the week, as in the 'sunshine-gram' mentioned earlier.

As these improvements continue, there will come a point when you and the pupil agree that it is time to move on to another level of responsibility.

TABLE 2.2   Checklist of progress

	Did I get my kit ready?	Did I try my best?
Tues 6 June	✗	✓
Thurs 8 June	✗	✗
Tues 13 June	✓	✗
Thurs 15 June	✗	✓
Tues 20 June	✓	✓
Thurs 22 June	✓	✓
Tues 27 June	✗	✗
Thurs 29 June	✓	✓
Tues 4 July	✓	✓
Thurs 6 July	✓	✗
Tues 11 July	✓	✗

To ascertain how the child measures up in the larger field of community responsibility, another simple self-report will provide the necessary baseline data that will help shape the next stage of developing responsibility (Table 2.3).

Again, the more 'yes' answers there are and the fewer 'no' answers there are indicate an increasing level of social responsibility, the ability and willingness to take on the responsibility for helping others and for being a positive influence in physical education lessons. Now the teacher could begin to devolve some of the responsibility for the lesson onto those pupils capable of accepting it in the appropriate manner. Group leadership, reciprocal teaching, coaching roles, and helping with clubs are all jobs that pupils can help with if they can demonstrate the required level of socially responsible maturity. The sport education model makes use of the multitude of roles that need to be filled in sporting situations and could be profitably used in this context. (To learn more about this curriculum model, see Siedentop, 1994.)

TABLE 2.3   My social responsibility

	Yes	No	Sometimes
1 I can work well with others			
2 I enjoy being part of a team			
3 I often help others in PE			
4 I help get out and put away the equipment			
5 I encourage my team-mates			

As this responsibility develops, teachers in other subjects should also notice an improvement in this aspect of the pupil's character. The research tells us that these traits learned in physical education do transfer to other areas of the curriculum. If needed, another checklist could be devised to measure the progress in social responsibility, although by this stage it may not be necessary.

A CASE STUDY: 'FAIR PLAY FOR KIDS'

There is now a body of research that demonstrates that these types of programmes and strategies work. Gibbons, Ebbeck and Weiss (1995) carried out a partial evaluation of a programme called 'Fair Play for Kids'. This is based on a teacher resource manual developed by the Commission for Fair Play in Canada (1990). The activities recommended to teachers in the manual are designed to promote attitudes and behaviours that exemplify fair play such as:

> (a) respect for the rules, (b) respect for officials and their decisions, (c) respect for opponents, (d) providing all individuals with an equal chance to participate, and (e) maintaining self-control at all times.
>
> (Gibbons, Ebbeck and Weiss, 1995: 247)

To test some strategies from the programme they used 452 boys and girls, from 18 Canadian elementary schools. They were from the fourth, fifth and sixth grade. It was decided to measure the children's scores in moral judgement, moral reasoning, moral intention and prosocial behaviours. A selection of teaching strategies was implemented over a seven-month period. These strategies included '*The problem-solving running shoe*', as discussed earlier, which is really a forum for conflict resolution. There were *relay games* in which ideas were shared with team-mates, and children learned to operate within the rules and to show self-control when things did not go well. The relay game was followed by a discussion on how well the strategy had worked. Lastly, there was something called '*improv*' (short for 'improvisation') in which children made up skits based on fair play scenarios given to them on cards. To measure whether or not these strategies were effective, there was a control group that received unchanged lessons in all subjects, an experimental group that was taught using the strategies only in physical education lessons, and another experimental group that was taught using the strategies in all their lessons. The pupils had either two or three physical education lessons a week, but the total time for physical education was 90 minutes for all groups.

The results from the study supported the hypothesis that a specially designed educational programme can bring about changes in targeted aspects of moral development. Both experimental groups had significant gains in their scores after the seven-month intervention phase. This supports the notion of transferability of learnt behaviours. Behaviour learnt in lessons such as social studies and fine arts can be demonstrated and observed across the curriculum. This also works the other way round and prosocial behaviour learnt in physical education can be seen in children in other areas of their everyday lives.

It should be stressed that most of the teacher strategies that were employed in this research were based on the structural-development theory of learning. This is based on interaction, so the children were given time to reflect on things that had happened in class and to act out scenarios that posed moral dilemmas. This imposes an additional problem of time available to conduct such activities. Teachers have little enough time available for their subject as it is and there may be some natural reluctance to give up what little time they have. For this reason it may be more appropriate to employ strategies that highlight the social learning aspects of behaviour promotion.

In a follow-up study, Gibbons and Ebbeck (1997) tested the effectiveness of social-learning teaching strategies as well as structural-development teaching strategies. These strategies were again taken from the 'Fair Play for Kids'programme. The researchers set out to compare the results of teaching strategies based on social-learning theory with teaching strategies based on structural-development theory.

There were 205 school children, in nine classes, taking part. The age range was the same as in the previous study. There was a control group (three classes) which was taught in a normal way, that is no teaching strategies from the 'Fair Play for Kids' programme, and two experimental groups. One of the experimental groups was taught with strategies using structural-development theory and the other was taught using social-learning theory teaching strategies. The social-learning theory strategies included *compliment cards* where pupils documented examples of fair play demonstrated by their classmates. These cards were collected and a few examples highlighted each week. A *fair play code* was used and posted in the gymnasium. This originated from pupil discussion on what constituted fair play. Lastly, *fair play agreements* were drawn up in which pupils identified certain behaviours that they would try to demonstrate during the course of their lessons. The teaching programme again lasted for seven months. Gibbons and Ebbeck used the same measures of moral judgement, moral reason, moral intention and prosocial behaviours with which to evaluate the programme.

Pupils benefited from both of the experimental teaching approaches when compared to those children in the control group. This again suggests that aspects of moral and prosocial behaviour can be learnt as a result of teaching interventions. The results indicate that the strategies based on structural-development brought about as much improvement as the strategies from a social-learning basis. Perhaps we should not be surprised at this. Teachers know that modelling and reinforcement are useful teaching strategies, but they are essentially teacher-based. It is a truism that children learn by doing and a programme that includes activities from a structural-development background allows this to happen. Interaction with each other, reflection on action and behaviour, and real engagement with the learning process are equally powerful learning agents.

This research indicates that teachers should adopt a wide range of teaching strategies from both social learning and structural-development backgrounds. This will enable teachers to demonstrate behaviours, and praise and encourage their pupils as well as providing opportunities for pupil involvement and engagement.

The results also indicate that moral development is not an automatic consequence of taking part in physical activity, but rather that a planned programme, structured and organised around the principles outlined in this book, and aimed at this area of affective development, can bring about desired changes in behaviour. In brief, when incorporated into a physical education programme, or indeed a school-wide programme, the teaching strategies in this new approach do make a difference.

Chapter 3 Assessing

THE THEORY

It would be unreasonable to burden teachers with cumbersome assessment procedures which add to the existing requirements. In recent times there has been an increasing demand for accountability and assessment. It would be easy to view this as all bad, but that would be to ignore the undoubted benefits of the place of assessment as part of the planning process, and the necessity of accountability in the education system.

It makes sense to point out that the effectiveness of the teaching can only be judged by measuring outcomes against previously set targets. Put simply, if we say that we will teach something, we need to be able to demonstrate that we really do teach it; and the only way to do that is by some form of assessment. It is relatively easy to measure cognitive and physical abilities. Objective tests, examinations and the collection of evidence all help to assess these areas. GCSEs and A-levels are fairly obvious examples of the measurement of cognitive skills. Teachers are also required to assess children's performance in physical education against the end of key stage descriptions. These reports should be annually updated. This will shortly be changed so that performances are measured against eight level descriptions, at least for Key Stages 1 to 3 (QCA, 1999b).

Although there are these general guidelines, affective outcomes are poorly served when it comes to assessment. National Curriculum (QCA, 1999c) and public examination requirements leave little opportunity for, nor do they offer any guidance on, the assessment or reporting of social and personal development in physical education. National Curriculum end of key stage descriptions in physical education offer only a general guide and have very few specific objectives against which pupils can be assessed (Carroll, 1994: 118).

Although the new level descriptions are more detailed, there is still very little mention of affective objectives, thus making contextual assessments extremely difficult.

Carroll (1994: 41–3) claims that the assessment of 'personal and social competencies and qualities' is problematic and fraught with difficulties. He rightly points out that there could be different interpretations of the same behaviours. That which is seen as independence by some people could be seen as selfishness by others, and what counts as leadership to some could be viewed as bossiness and dominance by others. Any assessment of these qualities must therefore be context-specific and explanatory rather than isolated and merely statistical. Comments such as 'Sarah shows good leadership skills when asked to coach a group through a practice' are more meaningful than 'Peter is a good leader; he showed fifteen instances of leadership in one lesson.' The first example sets the context for the comment and also for the characteristics that Sarah has demonstrated, whereas the second comment could very easily be interpreted to mean that Peter is a bossy boy who likes the sound of his own voice! This example shows that the problem is not only *what* to assess, but *how* to assess it. This chapter will deal with these issues.

The level descriptions of the attainment target in the proposed revised National Curriculum in physical education (QCA, 1999b) do not contain any references to personal and social (affective) outcomes. Teachers must therefore revert to the programmes of study for each of the key stages to identify what they should be assessing. There is a statement in the new NCPE that gives some overall indication of the importance of physical education and that statement does include some detail of the personal and social development that might be expected, although in very general terms.

> Physical education develops pupils' physical competence and confidence, and their ability to use these to perform in a range of activities. It promotes physical skilfulness, physical development and a knowledge of the body in action. Physical education provides opportunities for pupils to be creative, competitive and to face up to different challenges as individuals and in groups and teams. It promotes positive attitudes towards active and healthy lifestyles. Pupils learn how to think in different ways to suit a wide variety of creative, competitive and challenging activities. They learn how to plan, perform and evaluate actions, ideas and performances to improve their quality and effectiveness. Through this process pupils discover their aptitudes, abilities and preferences, and make choices about how to get involved in lifelong physical activity.
>
> (QCA, 1999c: 15)

This statement, although general, provides a useful indication of where teachers should be targeting their teaching of personal and social characteristics. Confidence building, being creative, working individually, working in groups and in teams, developing positive attitudes, discovering aptitudes and making choices are the minimum (in the affective domain) that is required from physical education in the NCPE. When this is put together with the framework for PSHE and the illustrated potential for physical education's contribution in that arena, teachers can very easily see that the affective characteristics that they can develop in pupils *and then assess* are quite considerable.

However, much of what teachers decide to assess will be determined by how individual schools and departments interpret the NCPE and the PSHE documents in their own schemes of work and their day-to-day teaching. This interpretation will, in turn, be grounded in the value that those schools and departments place on affective development. Schemes of work, units of work and lessons plans will all have aims and objectives listed in them. It is then up to teachers to assess how their pupils have developed in these areas and, by inference, how successful they have been in these aspects of their teaching.

Readers will be aware that a national curriculum, as well as being an educational statement, is a political statement. As governments are likely to change with the will of the people, so curricula can change and be changed. It is important therefore to realise that although government initiatives and curriculum developments make this new approach contextually apposite at the present time, the benefits of this new pedagogy are relevant to future incarnations of physical education curricula. The subject becomes expanded as it promotes the holistic development of the participants.

The two most commonly known types of assessment are *summative* assessment and *formative* assessment. 'The Theory' will also look at *ipsative* assessment, and will conclude with a review of *norm-referenced* and *criterion-referenced* assessment. We will now look at how these types of assessment can be used and whether they might have any applications in measuring the affective developments that we are aspiring to produce in our pupils.

Summative Assessment

As its name suggests, this type off assessment is based on a summation of evaluative procedures. It provides a summary of achievement. This type of assessment would in all probability be carried out at the end of a course of study or a unit of work. The purpose is to measure learning outcomes and report on them (Lambert, 1995: 269). The procedures are usually formal, with a proven record of reliability and validity. GCSEs, A-levels and pupil reports are summative assessments. Although it is possible that such assessments could be used diagnostically, or for planning purposes, it is more likely that such results will be for record-keeping, administration, policy-making and other bureaucratic uses. As such, they tend to serve the needs of politicians and administrators rather than the needs of the teachers and the children. Some summative assessments in the form of GCSEs and A-levels present strong barriers to educational progress. They are the gatekeepers of knowledge that allow or prevent access to further and higher education. In this way, they can be very important to children and young adults in schools.

Summative assessments are reported in school league tables and other types of league tables. They tell us how well a school, or a football team, has done in terms of results. They do not tell us about the experience of the education, or the experience of the football game. Did the school achieve good results but produce pupils who merely reproduce spoon-fed information? Did the football team grind out boring draws and one–nil wins at the expense of creative and attractive football? Summative assessment generally measures quantitative factors objectively. If a summative assessment were to be made of a personal and social characteristic, it could take the form of 'Harry has shown many more positive interactions this term. He can be relied upon to shake hands at the end of a game and he now takes responsibility for his own performance.' This type of statement tells us where Harry is now, at this given point in time. It also tells us something about his progress over the course of the term in personal and social behaviours. In this example, the evidence is the teacher's subjective opinion, which may or may not be accurate.

In summary, summative assessment procedures give a snapshot of the school's, individual's or team's performance. They can tell us something about progress, but they are not ideal for professional and educational purposes; they are an end in themselves.

Formative Assessment

In assessment terms, formative assessment can be viewed as the opposite to summative assessment. It is designed to inform on progress and status rather than to judge performance. Its nature is diagnostic in that formative assessment is used in planning future educational experiences. Formative assessment uses many procedures depending on what information is needed. These procedures range from the formal, as in norm-referenced tests, to informal, as in teacher-compiled checklists of social behaviour. Whereas summative assessment takes place at the end of a course, formative procedures take place at any time during the course, or unit of work, principally to inform the future direction of the work, and to give an indication of pupil progress. In this way, the assessment can be used to help teachers with their planning, or it can be used to help pupils by providing them with relevant feedback on their progress.

It can be seen from this brief description of formative assessment that it is principally of value to teachers and pupils. The purpose is mainly educational and professional rather than administrative. Formative assessments can be used

> 'It's great to see that there are many more positive social contacts than there were at the beginning of term, and I know that for some of you that has been very difficult, well done. But what about responsibility, I don't see any improvement, why is that?'
>
> There are one or two responses:
>
> 'Dunno, Miss',
>
> and then someone says:
>
> 'Well to be honest, Miss, I don't know when I could have been responsible, you always tell us exactly what to do.'

FIGURE 3.1   Formative assessment discussion

for many educational purposes. Let us assume that the affective objectives of a unit of work are to improve social interactions and increase self-responsibility. Halfway through the unit the teacher decides to see how the class is getting on. He or she uses a checklist in one lesson to record instances of positive social interaction and self-responsibility. At the end of the lessons he or she shares the results of this crude measurement with the class (Figure 3.1). A few minutes' discussion occurs and it transpires that the teacher has not devolved any responsibility to the class. He or she resolves to do this in future and then to assess progress again in a couple of weeks.

The assessment has been informal, brief, cooperative, diagnostic and formative. It took a little time in lesson to do the checklist and about five minutes for the discussion at the end of the lesson. This scenario has illustrated several educational possibilities. Progress has been evaluated, pupils have been involved in the process, objectives have been restated, a future direction has been defined, and both pupils and teacher know where they stand in relation to the overall pattern of the unit of work. Formative assessment has informed educational judgements and in this case it has positively influenced the educational process.

Formative assessments also provide a snapshot of educational progress, as do summative assessments, but crucially they should be used to change, refine and improve the teaching and learning process. They are not an end in themselves, merely a means to an end.

Ipsative Assessment

Ipsative assessment compares current performances with past performances on the same or similar tasks. Good examples of this are records of any sort. World records are ipsative assessments when they are improvements on past performances, as in track and field athletics, swimming, weight-lifting and so on. Similarly, improvements in school records are an ipsative measure of performance. This is also the case with personal bests. A pupil improving her 100 m time from 13.5 secs to 13.0 secs would make an ipsative assessment of her performance.

It is clear that this type of assessment favours the task-orientated sports person rather than the ego-orientated sports person. As such, this type of assessment is ideal for comparing the acquisition and improvement of social and personal characteristics. To measure whether one has done better than before, or to measure improvement on a personal aspect of behaviour, should only be measured ipsatively. Or rather, this type of measurement is the only one that provides *meaningful* evaluation in these areas. The measurement is not against a norm or even a criterion; rather it is a difference in personal behaviour that is the desired outcome.

Although records and personal bests are quantitative, objective and formal, and to a large degree uncontextual measures of performance, ipsative assessments can also be qualitative, subjective, informal and very much contextual. It may be that when dealing with personality traits, this is the only realistic way to assess improvement because of the imperative nature of the context. In the affective areas of personal and social development, children should only be measured, or assessed, against themselves. They, and the assessment, need to be task-orientated.

So, for a pupil who can relate cooperatively to only one or two friends within a class, the task would be for that pupil to expand his friendship circle to include two others with whom he can work in physical education. A reciprocal teaching strategy (pairs) could be extended to groups of three with each taking turns at the roles of coach and performers. Teacher talk and a reward system of merit marks leading to a certificate could be instituted. Gradual exposure to working with others, with the attendant reinforcement, would hopefully encourage our pupil to be more cooperative with others in the group. Our pupil would eventually be measured on his prior behaviour, he would be assessed on the task using ipsative assessment, and he would not have been compared to others. Children wither inside when they hear, 'Why can't you behave like Kate?' It is not only those misbehaving who wither, it can also be Kate! Obviously, a whole class would not be rearranged to benefit only one pupil. Increased cooperation, working with others and making new friends could be a realistic affective objective for a unit of work, and our example would easily fit under that umbrella objective.

Norm-referenced Assessment

This type of assessment is frequently used to rank pupils' work in comparison to the work of other pupils from the same group. The group might be as small as a class in a school or it might be as large as a whole population. For this type of assessment to work properly, there must be distinguishable differences between the subjects, or at least differences that can be recognised by the assessment instrument. If, for example, most of the pupils in a basketball class were about the same standard, it would be very difficult for there to be a teacher assessment that would place them in rank order in relation to the others in the group. Such an assessment would be unreliable. They would all be around the average ability for the group. If, however, the differences were large, from excelling to very low skilled, it would be easy for the teacher to make accurate assessments of individuals' rank positions within the group.

A further example of the use of norm-referenced assessment would be scoring pupils on a fitness test given to the group. The test would be fairly formally given and the results would be objective. Each child would have a score that would indicate his or her ability to perform a particular fitness task. The teacher would have scores for the whole group and it would therefore be fairly easy to generate group statistics such as mean scores, modal score, a median score and so on. Measuring the individual's score against the group statistic enables the teacher to make a norm-referenced assessment of that pupil's score. Pupils can then be ranked or ordered and the teacher will know which pupils would benefit from further fitness training, which ones are very fit, and which ones are close to the mean score. A further benefit is that it might be possible to place the group, and individual, scores against national norms, thus giving the teacher and the school an idea of where they stand in relation to the rest of the country, at least on that particular measure of fitness.

Of course, there are no national norms for personal and social behaviour. But a teacher will know what the norm is for any group that they teach. The teacher can then intuitively place any pupil in relation to that norm. However, such a judgement is unscientific and extremely subjective. Rather than use criterion-referenced (described later) or ipsative judgements, teachers do sometimes identify pupils in such a way, particularly in relation to unacceptable behaviour. The 'most poorly behaved'children in one group might be the norm in another group. Such judgements are contextually located and have little use in assessing and developing prosocial skill. It would be far better if children were encouraged to improve their own personal and social skills (ipsative) or aspire to a socially acceptable criterion for interactive behaviour (criterion-referenced).

Criterion-referenced Assessment

Criterion-referencing compares the work of individuals against a set of criteria. It is concerned with how an individual has performed, quite independently of how others have performed on the same task. Thus the quality of the individual's performance is assessed irrespective of the performance of other individuals. Pupils are not judged against each other as they are in norm-referenced assessment, they are judged against their performance on any set task.

Testing pupils in football to find out how many times they can each juggle a football before it falls to the ground is a criterion-referenced test, the criterion being their performance on the test. (However, if the teacher goes on to compare individual performances against group norms, such as mean score, this then becomes a norm-referenced test.) To expand the criterion-referenced example: the purpose of such a test or assessment could be to determine how well the pupils had mastered the skill of juggling, or to determine who needs extra time to practise (diagnostic), or maybe to select pupils above a certain score for football team training.

Another, perhaps a clearer, example is in track and field athletics where it is common to have standards of performance for which pupils are awarded points towards a cumulative award. The criterion of the standards covers a range of abilities and the pupils are being measured against the criterion, not against each other.

As mentioned earlier, where a standard of social and personal behaviour is communicated to the children and expected of them, the affective behaviours can be placed in comparison to that standard. So a teacher promoting sportsmanship might suggest at the beginning of a unit of work on badminton that he or she expected to see pupils congratulate each other after good shots and shake hands at the ends of games. The criteria are simple – the congratulations and shaking hands. The assessment is also simple – the teacher's observation of the pupils' performance of the criteria. The children either meet the criteria or they do not. What the teacher does next is dependent on the teaching strategy in place for developing these sportsmanship behaviours.

Summary

There is not one type of assessment that is best for assessing personal and social development in school children. Summative assessment might be used for end of key stage, or end of year reports. Formative assessment might be used during a unit of work to help the teacher and the pupils see how they are doing and to plan an effective way forward. Ipsative assessment is less threatening than other assessments and is probably best for informing pupils of their progress. Norm-referenced assessment places children in rank order and measures them against each other. It is hard to see the advantage of this in terms of affective outcomes for physical education. Criterion-referenced assessment allows pupils to reflect on their own performances, behaviours and abilities when compared to an agreed, or imposed, standard of behaviour. This means that they are being compared to an objective criterion, not ranked against their classmates.

THE PRACTICE

Methods of Assessment

A number of methods of assessment have already been tried and tested with some success. They measure different aspects of the physical education process. A brief consideration of each method will enable us to narrow the field to those that have real potential to help in the assessment of the affective dimension in physical education.

Practical Tests

These are obviously ideal for assessing skills and performances in practice and game play. Teachers would commonly give a test at the beginning of a unit and at the end of a unit to determine pupils' progress in the targeted physical skills. This type of assessment is not appropriate for affective outcomes. However, because we are dealing with a practical subject, it is likely, and desirable, that any assessment of the affective domain will be made in a practical situation. This is called 'authentic assessment', meaning that the assessment is located in a 'real context'.

Written Tests

Although it might be possible to ask pupils on a written test how they feel they have progressed in personal and social characteristics, these tests are usually used for measuring cognitive development. One group of written 'tests' that may prove useful are those 'tests' such as questionnaires, attitude scales and self-esteem instruments.

Examinations

These are similar to written tests and are mainly used in GCSE or A-level assessments. However, they are more formalised and conducted under examination conditions. As such, examinations in physical education are not very useful for assessing social and personal factors.

Oral Responses

Children's responses in question-and-answer sessions can certainly give a teacher an indication of their understanding of a topic, a practice or a skill. Similarly, if pupils are presented with situations that demand a response to do with sportsmanship, fairness or moral judgement in physical education, it is possible for the teacher to use such responses in making judgements about pupils' development in these areas.

Written Materials

Setting pupils essays, giving them worksheets to complete and other kinds of written work have not traditionally been a major part of the physical education lesson. Apart from the non-participants in a lesson, this type of work tends to detract too much from the time available for the motor content of the lesson. There is one type of written work that could be useful in assessing affective development and that is journal writing. This need not detract from lesson time and can be helpful in familiarising teachers with pupils' thoughts and feelings on the subject.

Video Recordings

The use of video recordings has a long history in research as a common method for investigating teacher behaviour and pupil behaviour. Such an objective 'eye' is ideal for observing pupil behaviour and interaction. It frees the teachers from the necessity of using checklists and the like in lessons, although it is time-consuming to review recordings at a later date.

Pupil Self-assessment

When used in conjunction with other assessment methods such as questionnaires or individual checklists or group discussion, pupil self-assessment may have some use. One of the problems associated with self-assessment is that the subjects have a tendency to see themselves as they would like to be seen. The use of self-assessment in isolation provides little of value to the teacher, apart from maybe the pupils' perception of their progress or status. This type of assessment must be used with another source, such as teacher observation.

Pupil Peer Assessment

Although peer assessment is part of reciprocal teaching and is to be encouraged in the psychomotor domain, allowing pupils to assess each other in the affective domain can be fraught with problems, unless combined with another method of assessment such as group discussion. Peer assessment merely produces one individual's opinion, or a group's opinion, of another individual. This summative type of opinion is not conducive to prosocial affective development and it may even be counter-productive. Asking non-participating pupils to collect data on checklists is different. They are not being asked to make a judgement on their peers, merely to record what happens. It can be seen that this type of data collection needs to be handled carefully to avoid pupil involvement in subjective judgements. Names could be omitted from such checklists, and only the behaviour instances recorded.

Group Discussion

If the boundaries of the discussion are clearly defined, and there are clear guidelines for the conduct of the discussion, group involvement of this kind can be most productive. These sessions can be used to establish objectives and purposes at the beginning of a unit, to check on progress, and to evaluate group progress and the effectiveness of the affective objectives programme at the end of a unit.

Teacher Observation

This can be interpreted in a number of ways, from a teacher casually watching a class and deducing that they are all playing fairly within the rules, to the implementation of a formalised observation schedule that targets certain behaviours of the pupils. If these schedules and checklists are used extensively they can be time-consuming and unwieldy, but careful and focused observation can provide information that allows teachers to effectively assess pupils in personal and social development.

This has been a subjective look at a variety of methods of assessment. This subjective interpretation has concluded that some are not suitable for dealing with the affective elements of physical education. However, written tests and materials, including limited self-assessment, group discussion and oral responses, and teacher observation including video recording, would appear to have some use in the assessment process. We will now look in more detail at each of these in turn.

Written Tests and Materials

The items discussed in this category are not 'tests' in the true sense of the word, that is they do not test the pupils, but are designed to find something out from the pupils. The type of 'test' can range from a questionnaire constructed by you to discover what are your pupils' perceptions of physical education, to a properly validated and reliable scale that measures pupils' self-esteem. The examples given here cover that full range.

Teacher Constructed Questionnaires

The questionnaire in Figure 3.2 is from the Manitoba 'Fair Play for Kids' programme. The items can obviously be amended to match what the teacher wants to find out. The example here would give an impression of how the pupils feel about physical education. Other questions could be asked to determine pupils' perception of the cognitive or physical elements of physical education lessons.

Results from such a questionnaire are not statistically significant and should only be used to inform the teachers about very specific situations. As such, they

Tick	My students:
	arrive on time for class
	say 'hello' to me in the hallway
	want to play and participate
	smile and laugh when they are in my class
	obey rules when I'm not watching them
	help out (even when they're not asked)
	take turns willingly
	put winning and losing into proper perspective
	realistically evaluate their own abilities
	want to learn
	think that physical education is important
	love physical education

FIGURE 3.2   Teaching affectively questionnaire

are context-specific, a crucial requirement of affective assessment according to Carroll (1994: 43). If a particular social characteristic is targeted for promotion in a unit of work, it could be that you give a questionnaire at the beginning and again at the end of the unit. This would enable a fairly crude form of assessment of progress to be carried out. This could then inform your planning and also perhaps the reporting.

Journals

The most common form of written materials referred to in the literature are journals. Like group discussions, they need to be focused to give any meaningful feedback on progress in the affective domain. In addition to being focused, they should not be an onerous task for the pupils to do. If time cannot be set aside daily for journal writing, then it should be possible to find a time at least once a week when pupils can have a few minutes to record their directed thoughts on a particular topic. Class teachers in primary schools may find that daily journal entries give a very good picture of the developmental process that their children are undergoing, in many areas of their educational progress. Because they encounter many teachers in the school day, it is likely that secondary school pupils will need to keep to subject-specific topics that they address in their journal entries.

Many benefits are possible with journal writing. Pupils can become reflectively involved in their own development through physical education, and their comments can provide you with much useful information that can then be used in your future lesson planning. In response to carefully framed questions, you can discover pupils' feelings about the class and how it is taught, pupils' ambitions and experiences and how the pupils think they are doing, and you can help pupils plan for their own progress and learning. Teachers can also gain information about their pupils' perceived progress which could be used in report writing. This could ease the time-consuming reporting process and provide real evidence that supports the view of the teacher.

Physical education lessons are very interactive settings and the journals should maintain this with teachers responding to the pupils' comments. Children appreciate this interaction and look forward to what you have to say.

In describing their experiences and promoting the value of journal writing, Cutforth and Parker (1996) offer some guidelines for teachers who may be considering using them with their classes.

Relate the question asked to the lesson/unit content. In the planning process, teachers will have determined objectives for each lesson. Ask questions that require responses to the objectives. If the affective objective was to promote

---

How was your behaviour today?

Good _____

OK   _____

Poor _____

Did you help anyone today?

Yes _____

No   _____

Figure 3.3 Simple response checklist

cooperation, ask how pupils have worked together, if they have helped each other, and what opportunities should they have in future lessons to achieve that objective. If the psychomotor objective was to improve receiving and sending the ball with their hands, as in basketball, ask whether the pupils thought they had improved, how did they know whether they had or not, and did they have much opportunity to practise the skill.

Decide on a format for journal writing. Pupils will find it quite difficult at first to be really reflective in their journal entries, so ask simple questions that require simple answers (Figure 3.3). Perhaps even give multiple-response checklists. As pupils get more accustomed to writing, they will be able to make more complex responses and the teacher's questions can become more probing and complex.

Formalise the actual writing time. Set aside the same time of day each week. For example, twice a week in their tutor groups, pupils could be asked to write up their journals; or perhaps they could write them at the end of their last physical education lesson of the week.

Respond to the pupils. If no teacher responses are forthcoming, the pupils will soon realise that they are doing work for work's sake. It is only fair that, having asked their opinions, teachers respond to them. It is this dialogue that teachers can use to personalise their comments and encourage and help pupils with their personal and social development. It will not be necessary to respond to every entry, but regular responses are essential. The feedback that this provides will give the pupils an ongoing commentary on their progress. Teachers can use their responses to encourage, advise, chastise, help and prompt their pupils. In return, pupils feel that they are being listened to and receiving individual treatment from the teacher.

Self-esteem Measures

There is a long history of claims that participation in sports, physical activity and physical education is beneficial to self-esteem. However, such participation is only beneficial if certain criteria are met. Children must have a realistic chance of success, they must be judged on the task performance, they must value what they are doing and they must receive positive feedback from peers and significant others (see the section on ipsative assessment on pp. 58–9).

In addition to this, it must be recognised that old measures of global self-esteem only give a broad picture to which there are many contributory factors. The newer multi-dimensional model has more appeal because one can assess self-esteem in different facets of one's existence. So one could possibly get a measure of self-esteem in social settings, an intellectual self-esteem and a physical self-esteem. This is a step in the right direction, but it does not allow for children placing different values on differing aspects of their selves. This is where a hierarchical model is the most realistic and powerful concept. Each contributory component of self-esteem is made up of sub-components, which in turn are constituted by even smaller components, and so on. The beauty of this model is that it allows individuals to construct a model of self-esteem based on those aspects of their personality and self on which they place most value.

A measure of physical self-esteem is needed to enable teachers to determine whether their programme is making a contribution to the self-esteem of their pupils. The instrument shown in Figure 3.4 is the Children's Physical Self-Perception Profile (Whitehead, 1995). The profile has sections that measure an individual's perception of their sports competence, global self-worth (Harter, 1985), physical stamina, body attractiveness, physical self-worth and physical strength. When taken together, these provide a measure of physical self-perception.

When administering the profile, first ask the children to decide which statement best matches them. Then they should go to the side of that statement and decide if it is just 'sort of true' or 'really true'. They should put a tick in that box. Explain the instructions and point out that there are no correct or incorrect answers.

ID#: _____ Age: _____ Grade: _____ Boy or Girl (circle)

WHAT I AM LIKE

Really True for me	Sort of True for me				Sort of True for me	Really True for me
1. ☐	☐	Some kids do very well at all kinds of sports	BUT	Other kids *don't* feel they are very good when it comes to sports	☐	☐
2. ☐	☐	Some kids feel *uneasy* when it comes to doing vigorous physical exercise	BUT	Other kids feel *confident* when it comes to doing vigorous physical exercise	☐	☐
3. ☐	☐	Some kids feel that they have a good-looking (fit-looking) body compared to other kids	BUT	Other kids feel that compared to most, their body *doesn't* look so good	☐	☐
4. ☐	☐	Some kids feel that they *lack* strength compared to other kids their age	BUT	Other kids feel that they are stronger than other kids their age	☐	☐
5. ☐	☐	Some kids are *proud* of themselves physically	BUT	Other kids *don't* have much to be proud of physically	☐	☐
6. ☐	☐	Some kids are often *unhappy* with themselves	BUT	Other kids are pretty *pleased* with themselves	☐	☐
7. ☐	☐	Some kids wish they could be a lot better at sports	BUT	Other kids feel that they are good enough at sports	☐	☐
8. ☐	☐	Some kids have a lot of stamina for vigorous physical exercise	BUT	Other kids soon get out of breath and have to slow down or quit	☐	☐
9. ☐	☐	Some kids find it *difficult* to keep their bodies looking good physically	BUT	Other kids find it *easy* to keep their bodies looking good physically	☐	☐
10. ☐	☐	Some kids think that they have stronger muscles than other kids their age	BUT	Other kids feel that they have weaker muscles than other kids their age	☐	☐
11. ☐	☐	Some kids don't feel very confident about themselves physically	BUT	Other kids really feel good about themselves physically	☐	☐

FIGURE 3.4   Children's Physical Self-Perception Profile

	Really True for me	Sort of True for me				Sort of True for me	Really True for me
12.	☐	☐	Some kids are *happy* with themselves as a person	**BUT**	Other kids are often *not* happy with themselves	☐	☐
13.	☐	☐	Some kids think they could do well at just about any new sports activity they haven't tried before	**BUT**	Other kids are afraid they might *not* do well at sports they haven't ever tried	☐	☐
14.	☐	☐	Some kids *don't* have much stamina and fitness	**BUT**	Other kids have *lots* of stamina and fitness	☐	☐
15.	☐	☐	Some kids are *pleased* with the appearance of their bodies	**BUT**	Other kids wish that their bodies looked in better shape physically	☐	☐
16.	☐	☐	Some kids *lack* confidence when it comes to strength activities	**BUT**	Other kids are very confident when it comes to strength activities	☐	☐
17.	☐	☐	Some kids are very *satisfied* with themselves physically	**BUT**	Other kids are often *dissatisfied* with themselves physically	☐	☐
18.	☐	☐	Some kids *don't* like the way they are leading their life	**BUT**	Other kids *do* like the way they are leading their life	☐	☐
19.	☐	☐	In games and sports some kids usually *watch* instead of play	**BUT**	Other kids usually *play* rather than watch	☐	☐
20.	☐	☐	Some kids try to take part in energetic physical exercise whenever they can	**BUT**	Other kids try to *avoid* doing energetic exercise if they can	☐	☐
21.	☐	☐	Some kids feel that they are *often* admired for their good-looking bodies	**BUT**	Other kids feel that they are *seldom* admired for the way their bodies look	☐	☐
22.	☐	☐	When strong muscles are needed, some kids are the *first* to step forward	**BUT**	Other kids are the *last* to step forward when strong muscles are needed	☐	☐
23.	☐	☐	Some kids are *unhappy* with how they are and what they can do physically	**BUT**	Other kids are *happy* with how they are and what they can do physically	☐	☐
24.	☐	☐	Some kids *like* the kind of person they are	**BUT**	Other kids often wish they were someone else	☐	☐
25.	☐	☐	Some kids feel that they are *better* than others their age at sports	**BUT**	Other kids *don't* feel they can play as well	☐	☐

FIGURE 3.4   (continued)

70

Really True for me	Sort of True for me			Sort of True for me	Really True for me
26. ☐	☐	Some kids soon have to quit running and exercising because they get tired	**BUT** Other kids can run and do exercises for a long time without getting tired	☐	☐
27. ☐	☐	Some kids are *confident* about how their bodies look physically	**BUT** Other kids feel *uneasy* about how their bodies look physically	☐	☐
28. ☐	☐	Some kids feel that they are *not* as good as others when physical strength is needed	**BUT** Other kids feel that they are among the *best* when physical strength is needed	☐	☐
29. ☐	☐	Some kids have a positive feeling about themselves physically	**BUT** Other kids feel somewhat negative about themselves physically	☐	☐
30. ☐	☐	Some kids are very *happy* being the way they are	**BUT** Other kids wish they were *different*	☐	☐
31. ☐	☐	Some kids *don't* do well at new outdoor games	**BUT** Other kids are *good* at new games right away	☐	☐
32. ☐	☐	When it comes to activities like running, some kids are able to keep on going	**BUT** Other kids soon have to quit to take a rest	☐	☐
33. ☐	☐	Some kids *don't* like how their bodies look physically	**BUT** Other kids are *pleased* with how their bodies look physically	☐	☐
34. ☐	☐	Some kids think that they are strong, and have good muscles compared to other kids their age	**BUT** Other kids think that they are weaker, and *don't* have such good muscles as other kids their age	☐	☐
35. ☐	☐	Some kids wish that they could feel better about themselves physically	**BUT** Other kids *always* seem to feel good about themselves physically	☐	☐
36. ☐	☐	Some kids are *not* very happy with the way they do a lot of things	**BUT** Other kids think the way they do things is *fine*	☐	☐

FIGURE 3.4   (continued)

When scoring the test, some questions are 'reverse-scored', with different values from 1 to 4 or from 4 to 1 being allotted to the ticks placed in the boxes relating to each question, so be sure to follow the matrix below:

Questions 1, 3, 5, 8, 10, 12, 13, 15, 17, 20, 21, 22, 24, 25, 27, 29, 30, 32, 34
Score 4 − 3 − 2 − 1

BUT:

Questions 2, 4, 6, 7, 9, 11, 14, 16, 18, 19, 23, 26, 28, 31, 33, 35, 36
Score 1 – 2 – 3 – 4

As indicated earlier, there are sub-scales within the overall measure, and different items within the overall measure constitute these sub-scales. These sub-scales are made up as indicated below:

Perceptions of one's:

Sport competence	items 1,	7,	13,	19,	25,	31
Physical stamina	items 2,	8,	14,	20,	26,	32
Body attractiveness	items 3,	9,	15,	21,	27,	33
Physical strength	items 4,	10,	16,	22,	28,	34
Physical self-worth	items 5,	11,	17,	23,	29,	35
Global self-worth	items 6,	12,	18,	24,	30,	36

You might decide that you only want to discover your pupils' feelings of physical self-worth or sport competence. In these cases you could use only the relevant portions of the instrument. However, you should be warned that the use of separate components in this way has not been tested for validity, reliability or effect. So the results obtained might not give a completely accurate representation of your pupils' perceptions. Nevertheless, you would get an idea of how they felt, it just would not have any statistical credibility.

When using the instrument, obviously, the higher the score, the higher the pupil's perception of physical self. As a single score it merely indicates high, medium or low perceptions. But used as a 'before and after' type of measure, you would be able to see changes in scores over the course of a unit of work, a school year, or indeed, any time span. However, if you wanted to operate this as an experiment, there would need to be a control group which you taught in the normal way. There would also need to be an experimental group who were taught using the new approach. Any changes in the scores of the experimental group would then be a result of the new teaching approach.

Group Discussions and Oral Responses

In political circles these would be called 'focus groups', 'focus' being the important word. A group discussion, particularly with younger children, can very easily lose its way if it is not focused on certain topics. Let us look at an example of how this might work.

A group is doing a unit of work in volleyball; the personal and social characteristic targeted is democratic decision making. At the beginning of the unit the teacher explains that a group will be elected to discuss progress at intervals during the unit. The class holds an election of perhaps six representatives. It would be up to you, the teacher, to ensure that those elected were representative of the class. Meetings of the group could be held after the physical education lessons or in tutor group time. The first meeting might be after the second week and the topic of discussion could be whether everyone in the class understands the objectives set out and how they should work to achieve them. This type of feedback enables you to check on progress and possibly amend future lessons accordingly. The second meeting might be halfway through the unit and the discussion could revolve around whether the objectives are being met, what opportunities are being given to practise democratic decision making, and what better opportunities could be made available. A final meeting could be held at the end of the unit. This summative meeting would review the whole process, assess group and programme progress (any assessment of individual progress must remain with you), and make recommendations for future units of this type. The group discussion method is an example of democracy at work and, as such, it fits this scenario very well. Efforts must be made to ensure that the pupils talk to their representatives and that the class representatives report accurately on the class feelings and concerns.

An added benefit of this group discussion method is that it encourages pupils to feel that they can make a difference to their education, that they can influence what happens in their physical education lessons and therefore they will have a vested interest in the accomplishment of the unit's objectives. They will develop a modified 'ownership' of the lessons and of the whole process. It has already been pointed out that teachers must believe in what they are trying to achieve; if pupils believe in it also, the chances of success are much increased.

Teacher Observations and Video Recordings

Teacher observations, including video recordings, will be context-related (as recommended by Carroll, 1994: 43) because they will have occurred in real lessons and not in isolated, or experimental, circumstances. Assessments and observations made in this way are *authentic assessments*, in that they are assessments of pupils applying 'skills and knowledge to solve "real world" problems, giving them a sense of authenticity' (Lund, 1997: 25). This adds considerably to the quality of the assessment, and assessments made in this way can be used for evaluating teaching effectiveness as well as for detailing progress and achievement of individuals.

Having established the authenticity of the observation and the method, teachers need to develop a way of interpreting what they see. Many options are available including checklists, frequency counts, coding schedules and other interaction analysis instruments. (For a comprehensive account of available instruments see Darst, Zakrajsek and Mancini, 1989.) It is likely that some teachers will want to be quite specific in what they observe, and none of the existing instruments is able to meet their requirements. There is no reason why teachers should not design their own recording and organising instrument as long as a few guidelines are adhered to.

The Process of Designing an Instrument

Decide and define what is to be observed. This may sound self-evident, but problems can arise if there is not a clear idea of what one is looking for. To merely say that 'I'm going to look for social interaction' is too broad a statement. How will this interaction be manifested? Will non-verbal actions like smiles count or will only verbal interactions be counted? It is better to be more specific and identify very clearly what will be recorded, for example 'I'll record non-verbal, social interactions as demonstrated by smiles, grimaces, thumbs-up, clapping and other physical gestures both positive and negative.' It is possible, of course, to identify a number of qualities to be recorded and, as long as they are clearly defined, this is quite acceptable.

Design a chart on which the recording can be made. The chart here (Figure 3.5) is easily adaptable to many uses. Essential information about the class goes at the top. The affective trait to be observed is noted, in our example, 'social interaction'. If you are experimenting with teaching for affective development, you may well have a *treatment* group that you are working with, and a *control* group that is being taught in the normal way – although this is not absolutely necessary to determine affective development in pupils. A limited number of subjects can be observed at any one time and their names are recorded down the side. Names should only be used for teacher observations. If children, such as non-participants, are doing the recording, then they should merely record instances of the targeted behaviours (see Figure 3.6: helping, encouraging, equipment/assistance). This avoids any personal, subjective judgements being made by their peers. The observer then watches the lesson or videotape and records the various interactions made by these pupils in the rows across the chart. So a N is recorded for a positive non-verbal interaction, a circled V for a negative verbal interaction and so on.

Interpret the data. A cumulative total of each type of interaction recorded gives the teacher some minimal information. When comparing the same pupil in different lessons, one could say something like 'John showed more positive,

Date: _____   Recorder: _____   Unit of Work: _____   Lesson Length: _____

Affective Trait: _____   Treatment or Control (circle)   V: Verbal
N: Non-verbal
(circle if negative)

Class: _____

Object	Coding	Totals	Proportions

FIGURE 3.5   Affective traits chart

non-verbal social interactions in lesson B than in lesson A', or 'John showed more positive, non-verbal social interactions than Sarah'. These types of statements tell us nothing about John's development. It would be better to work out the instances of positive, non-verbal social interactions as a proportion of the total social interactions recorded and compare this proportion over a series of lessons, or at least two lessons separated by a period of time. One could then get an idea of John's progress, or otherwise, in the area of a specific social interaction, reporting that 'John has shown improvement in the way he relates to his peers as demonstrated by an increase in the proportion of positive, non-verbal interactions in lessons.'

Video Recordings

These are merely a tool to aid the process of teacher observation. Teachers set themselves many tasks within any one lesson such as the actual teaching, managing large groups of pupils, refereeing a game or games, monitoring learning, continually assessing motivation and participation, and ensuring a safe environment, both physically and emotionally, for their pupils. In some instances, the addition of the necessity to record or observe personal and social characteristics of pupils would not be a realistic proposition. The use of a video recording of a lesson, taken through a wide-angled lens, enables the teacher to make the required observations at a later time. It would not be an economical use of time for video recordings to be used solely for evaluating personal and social characteristics of pupils. Teachers also need to evaluate and report on other areas of progress within the subject, notably physical performance. The use of videotape therefore allows teachers to make these different evaluations in the secure knowledge that the evidence is real and relatively permanent.

Pupils will initially be fascinated by the use of the video-recorder and will behave in atypical ways. However, they will soon become accustomed to its use and behaviour will quickly return to normal. When viewing the tapes, the teacher will be seeing behaviour in a naturalistic setting, and therefore the assessment will be authentic.

Checklists

A good example of this recording method is the Lesson Observation Sheet. The advantage of this method is that it does not necessarily involve the teacher in the actual recording. If children are asked to do the recording, the disadvantage is that it relies on their accuracy and honesty. Pupils who are sitting out the lesson for one reason or another (illness, lost kit, etc.) watch the lesson and record incidents of behaviours (positive) that occurred as the lesson progressed.

Class.......................................Date.............................
Helping ✓ 44
Encouraging ✓ 49
Equipment/Assistance ✓ ✓ ✓ ✓ ✓ ✓ ✓ ✓ ✓ ✓ ✓ ✓ 12

FIGURE 3.6 Lesson observation sheet

In the example in Figure 3.6 these behaviours are identified as helping a friend, encouraging a teammate and assisting with equipment.

If you have stipulated behavioural expectations before the lesson, these observations could provide the basis for feedback and discussion. Emphasis on the positive is more useful than identifying the negative, although you will undoubtedly have noticed any negative behaviour that has occurred. Obviously, the recorders may become distracted or not interpret behaviours accurately. Such results would only give a crude indication of what is happening in the lesson. For a more accurate result, you would need to do the recording yourself, either in the lesson or from a videotape of the lesson. The results from such checklists can be formulated to give information in the form of frequency counts.

This is one of the easiest ways of recording and then organising the information – to simply count the instances of the behaviours being observed. By comparing frequencies of certain behaviours over a period of time, it is possible to see trends of behaviour change in pupils. This will give teachers information which can be used to judge the effectiveness of the teaching and also the development of the pupils, thus allowing an assessment of affective development to be made.

Computer Coding

The 'performance pedagogy' school of research in the 1980s and early 1990s produced a wealth of coding schedules that were useful in analysing teacher and pupil behaviours. Many of these were later adapted for use with laptop computers, thus allowing 'live coding' in physical education lessons. In general these instruments recorded teacher and pupil 'technical' behaviours that were limited to the instruction and management aspects of the lessons. A few, however, were designed to record other aspects of lessons (Darst, Zakrajsek and Mancini, 1989).

One of the most adaptable of these is the Physical Education Teacher Assessment Instrument (PETAI) (Phillips, Carlisle, Steffen and Stroot, 1986). Its title describes only a quarter of its potential. As well as recording what teachers do, it can also be used to record pupil behaviours; and, more importantly, it can be programmed to record up to 18 pupil and teacher behaviours that can be selected by the investigator/researcher. This allows the recorder to enter personal and social behaviours which are not otherwise recorded by the PETAI. Each affective behaviour that is entered into the program has a key assigned to it. So a teacher may decide to look at pupils in terms of cooperation, teamwork and encouraging others, and also look at the teacher's encouragement and humorous comments to pupils. As the recorder watches the lesson, or videotape, he or she presses the relevant keys that denote the pupil and teacher behaviours. The computer then records the total time, and the percentage of lesson time, spent in these behaviours. When taken at different times during a unit of work, these results would give a clear indication of the development of these selected behaviours.

As with the results of other types of assessment instruments, the use to which they are put will vary. Some teachers will record them and use them for reports, some will use them to assess personal and social development in their pupils and others will use the results to evaluate and possibly change the content of their units of instruction. The results could, of course, be used for all of these and other purposes.

Summary

Assessment of the affective dimension of pupils' development in physical education has historically received very little, if any, attention. This chapter has described some of the ways that teachers can assess this affective domain in physical education. We have looked at a variety of written tests and materials including journals, oral reporting, particularly group discussion, and teacher observations including video recording. These are the most 'user friendly' instruments of assessment in this area and are fairly easily administered without the need to resort to statistical analysis. In some ways this is a weakness, in that the results generated cannot be used in generalising to a larger population. On the other hand, it could be viewed as a strength, in that the results are context-specific and relate very closely to naturalistic settings, that is they describe what is really happening in real-life situations.

It is quite likely that you will want to adapt or invent your own ways of measuring personal and social development, and the key principles to be considered in this endeavour have been reviewed here. In this way, you can plan your own units of work, set your own objectives and discover whether you have been successful in this aspect of your teaching.

A CASE STUDY

There have not been many instances of assessments of affective outcomes from physical education lessons. As one writer put it, 'How do you measure a rainbow?' (Carlson, 1982: 1), and many other writers have commented that these outcomes are notoriously difficult to measure. As mentioned earlier, very little is offered in the way of guidelines, and curriculum documents are not very helpful when it comes to determining what we should assess. Nevertheless, there is an obligation for teachers to assess what they claim to teach, and the purpose of this book is to enable teachers to teach physical education for social and personal development. A number of anecdotal reports and subjective hearsay evidence have provided an indication of the effect of these programmes, but this does not provide significant evidence of their success. One of the most important studies that has assessed affective outcomes, and provided the evidence to support the efficacy of specific curricular intervention, was conducted by Sharpe, Brown and Crider (1995).

Sharpe, Brown and Crider set out to test the effects of a primary school physical education curriculum which primarily focused on the prosocial behaviours in team sport activities. The researchers hoped to reduce conflict and off-task behaviour and increase leadership and independent conflict resolution The teaching strategies used for the promotion of these behaviours were teacher talk at the beginning of each lesson, defining certain character traits for each lesson (enthusiasm, peer respect, etc.), assigning varying roles to pupils and delegating some responsibility, and verbal and written feedback, to the teams after each lesson. The researchers used two classes who were taught using the programme and one control class over the course of a series of lessons. The lessons were videotaped and the identified behaviours were computer coded. Frequency counts were produced from these data and these frequencies were plotted on graphs. This simple process enabled them to make a judgement as to the efficacy of their sportsmanship curriculum programme.

Videotaping of lessons is a useful technique because it provides a relatively permanent record of the lessons. In this instance, the researchers were looking at particular aspects of behaviour, but teachers could just as easily have used the videotapes for assessing pupils' game play, skill development, instances of performance feedback, or any number of factors that constitute the content of a physical education lesson.

The use of a computer for coding the behaviour and occurrences in physical education lessons has a long history in pedagogical research. Obviously, this coding could be done by hand, but this is very time consuming. These coding instruments are tools which can very easily give a quantitative account of the lesson. If the instrument can be fine tuned to record affective behaviours (as with the PETAI), then this fulfils the needs of our assessment requirements.

Using the frequency counts and graphs provided a visual form of results that was very easy to interpret. From these results, Sharpe, Brown and Crider were able to determine that the programme produced no decrease in conflict behaviour. However, the results did show that independent conflict resolution and leadership behaviours increased, and the number of off-task behaviours decreased, as a result of the prosocial behaviour programme. Because of this decrease in off-task behaviour, pupils spent more time engaged with the instructional content of the lesson. The researchers also recorded that these findings from physical education lessons were mirrored in regular classroom lessons.

It would be relatively simple for practising physical education teachers to adopt this technique of frequency counts and depiction of the results on graphs with their own classes. There are usually some non-participants in most physical education classes, and these pupils could be required to keep a record of targeted behaviours using the frequency count charts shown earlier in this section. Merely recording the behaviour and not identifying individual pupils would avoid any personality conflicts within the class. The teacher could then display the resultant graphs to show the class how their social and personal characteristics are developing throughout the course of a unit of work. In fact, the raw data of the frequency counts could be used in mathematics lessons to generate the graphs. In this way, physical education would be making a contribution to a cross-curricular initiative and the teacher would not have spent any time in recording, interpreting or assessing. However, having made the assessment, there is a professional obligation to use that information to reflect on practice and consider refinements, possibly amendments, to the programme. Another advantage of this type of assessment recording is that it takes place in an authentic, or real, location and provides objective, concrete evidence of personal and social development. The teacher can use this to comment on pupil progress in the required reporting procedure.

The reporting of this research study shows that a multitude of assessment methods can be used to produce the evidence that teachers need. Each method naturally produces different types of data which can be used for a variety of ends. While not advocating that busy teachers replicate what has been described here, it has been shown that at least some of the assessments can be adopted and used in real-life situations. In the case study described here of pupil recorders and cross-curricular cooperation, this would be relatively easy to manage and not too burdensome for already overstretched physical education teachers.

Chapter 4   Reflecting

THE THEORY

The Reflective Practitioner

Although there have been many interpretations of reflective practice, a
common thread runs through them all. This thread is best summed up in one
word: thinking. Reflective practice involves thinking. Sometimes this will be
thinking about one's values, sometimes about one's problems, sometimes about
the implications of one's practice; but thinking must be central to the reflection
process. This thinking should not be just a commentary on teaching. 'That went
well, I think I'll try that again tomorrow' is not reflective practice. But 'That went
well, what was it about my teaching that caused that to happen?' is reflective
practice. In this way teachers problematise their teaching. This is not to say that
their teaching is a problem, just that it encourages teachers to pose a problem
(ask a question) which they can then attempt to answer by reflecting on a variety
of answers. In truth, 'reflexive practice' is a better term in that a reflex is a
response, and reflection is, in general use, a mirror image, a replication of
practice. We will maintain the more common terminology of reflection and,
while recognising the inadequacies of the term, accept that it has an agreed
currency in common use.

In a more fundamental way, reflection helps teachers develop into
intellectuals as opposed to being technicians (Ball, 1995). This is part of a
contemporary move away from a positivist, linear approach to teaching. This
linear approach encourages teachers to work in a very prescribed way, as in the
NCPE. The process of reflection, and Ball in his writing, encourage teachers to
recognise that teaching is far more than prescription; that it involves a personal,
social construction of the educational encounter, the pedagogical moment. It is

not possible, nor desirable, to 'throw the baby out with the bathwater', that is to get rid of the NCPE. But let us recognise that it has its limitations and teachers, as reflective intellectuals, can achieve a great deal to counter those limitations.

Reflective teachers are those who look back on their work, their teaching and their pupils' learning, and reconstruct what happened and why. They then propose alternatives and take into account the social, moral and political contexts that surround their teaching and schooling in general. Thus, the subject content cannot be separated from the context in reflective teaching. This factor is the main strength of reflective teaching; it has the potential to make the subject far more relevant to the pupils' experience because it takes into account the experiential nature of the physical education curriculum.

Teachers who can reflect on their own practice are more likely to enhance their professional development than those teachers who just teach their lessons and carry out little in the way of lesson evaluation, assessment of their teaching, or self-reflection. Obviously, this reflection needs to be guided in the earlier stages of professional development. Students, student teachers and beginning teachers need to know what aspects of teaching and learning to reflect upon. Therefore, part of initial teacher education (ITE), and continuing professional development (CPD) (possibly induction) for beginning teachers, must provide a knowledge base of values, goals, content and educational practices within which teachers can locate their reflections. They will also need guidance on *how* to go about reflecting on their practice. Some of this guidance is given later in this book. One of the advantages of reflective practice is that it is entirely context-specific. It is not abstract theory that does not appear to have any practical application.

Capel, Leask and Turner (1995: 255) use action research as the defining characteristic of a reflective practitioner. They suggest that, just as teachers should be concerned with pupil learning, so they should be similarly concerned with their own learning as demonstrated by their improved practice. Action research involves the identification of an area of investigation, the collection of data, possibly observations in a naturalistic setting, the analysis of the data, and the implementation of changes that may be suggested as a result of the research. This framework imposes a fairly narrow interpretation of reflective practice. It limits reflective practice to those areas under investigation, whereas reflective practice is something that teachers should do almost as an accepted part of their everyday professional lives. Perhaps it would be more realistic to suggest the relationship in the reverse order – that reflection is a necessary component of action research. Nevertheless, the two are closely linked.

In its broadest definition, reflective practice requires teachers to question their values and their practice. The first question is, 'Is what I am teaching worthwhile, is it of value?' To a large degree this question is answered for us because most teachers work within a curriculum framework that has already decided what is worth teaching. The NCPE is a good example of this. The second question therefore assumes paramount importance: 'Is what I'm doing working?' (Hellison and Templin, 1991: 3). This leads on to many other questions, such as 'What did the children learn today?', 'Is there a better way of structuring my lesson to achieve my learning objective?', 'How did the children feel when they left my lesson?' The truthful answers to these and many other questions will provide teachers with information on which to base judgements about their teaching. Sometimes the answers will be uncomfortable, but only by asking such questions and by discovering the truth, will teachers be able to improve their practice by reflecting on it. In addition to these pragmatic questions, teachers should also be asking political, social and moral questions such as 'Whose values am I promoting if I only teach competitive, male, team games?', 'Would these children benefit from learning the social rules and etiquette of cricket, or should I just teach them the skills?' and 'How can I structure this outdoor pursuits experience so that my pupils will encounter, and hopefully deal with, a moral dilemma?'

Reflection needs to be focused. By answering specific questions, student teachers and teachers can avoid trying to reflect on all aspects of their teaching, and the pupils' learning, at once. An approach that questions all aspects of the pedagogy is similar to a teacher overloading a pupil with performance feedback when trying to improve the performance of a skill. By focusing on one or two aspects of that skill, the pupil is more likely to absorb the relevant feedback information. Similarly, teachers will be better able to reflect productively on their performance if they are selective with the focus of their reflection. Some suggestions for focusing reflective questioning are given later.

The foregoing assumes that reflective practice is a 'good thing' and if one accepts that becoming a more professionally complete teacher is a desirable outcome, then it is indeed a 'good thing'. However, there are dangers. By asking ourselves deep, probing and sometimes personal questions about our practice and our existence as educators, we are exposing ourselves to the possibility that we might not like, or feel comfortable with, the answers that we give. This self-analysis can expose deep-seated prejudices and unfounded pedagogical assumptions. For example, one may have always held an assumption that, in spite of all the talk of gender equity in physical education and sports, in reality, boys are better suited to competitive team games and girls are more suited to individual and aesthetic activities. This type of finding would cause one to completely redefine one's view of physical education.

Risk is uncomfortable and scary. Why put ourselves into potentially uncomfortable situations when we could carry on as we are? Well, that is the alternative – to maintain the status quo and to carry on in the same old way. But reflective practice and reflective teaching are about challenging the status quo, and the way it has always been, in search of a better way, to achieve a different approach. Reflective practice is a mechanism that encourages and assists teachers and educators to make progress. The whole thrust of this book is about a different approach, an alternative way. Reflection is therefore an essential part of the proposed programme and process. (For more in-depth accounts of the theoretical background to reflective practice, readers should look at Kirk, 1986 and Schon, 1987.)

THE PRACTICE

The methods of practical reflection described here are very closely related and use the same questioning techniques. The first, journal keeping, is probably more appropriate for pre-service teachers or newly qualified teachers (NQT). It is more formal, provides a more concrete framework, and takes more time to accomplish. It allows the student or the NQT to make a permanent record of the basis for their reflections and to track their developing professional expertise.

Self-reflective questioning, the second method, can be individually or collaboratively undertaken. The use of a 'critical friend' (a professional, experienced colleague who is trusted to be honest, sympathetic and knowledgeable) is an enabling device to help the subject of the reflection address the process effectively and adequately. Individual reflection is the most difficult to achieve, because one has to be aware of what questions need asking and also what constitutes an effective answer.

From a professional, developmental point of view it is probably best to progress from journal writing, to collaborative reflection and on to individual reflection as one's career evolves. In each case, the secret of effective reflection is focusing that reflection.

Topics of Focus

Zeichner and Tabachnick (1991) use four topics as focuses for reflection: the student (pupil), the teaching strategies, the subject matter and social and political issues. Although I suggest that the reader use these four topics, I would add a fifth – one's own practice of teaching. This practice is not only limited to the technical notion of strategy. It is a more personal interpretation of the teaching act. It is to do with *how* one teaches and is also about style of teaching.

The focus on *the pupil* (Figure 4.1) naturally recognises that the end product of teaching should be learning and that effective teaching should be aimed at that outcome. Learning includes the process as well as the outcomes of education. This topic should also allow reflection on the experiential nature of education – how the pupil has related to learning and what the experience of learning has meant to the pupil. These are some of the questions that you might use to begin your reflection using the pupils as a focus.

Did my pupils learn what I set out to teach them?

Did they enjoy the experience?

Did I make the lesson meaningful to them?

If they didn't learn what I wanted, what was the reason for that?

In what ways did their learning develop their social and personal skills?

FIGURE 4.1 Pupil experience

When deciding which *teaching strategies* (Figure 4.2) to use in one's lessons, a teacher will have gone through a kind of pre-reflection process. (Refer back to Chapter 2 to read how this happens.) The purpose of reflecting on teaching strategies is to analyse in depth the effectiveness of those strategies in achieving one's objectives. These few questions also point to the planning process that you will have carried out prior to teaching the lesson.

What did I expect to achieve with that strategy?

Could I have used another strategy more effectively?

Would I do the same lesson again to achieve the same affective aims?

Can I invent another similar strategy?

Did I get the pupils' feedback on how the strategy worked?

FIGURE 4.2 Teaching strategies

The question of *subject matter* (Figure 4.3) arises from the NCPE, the schemes, and units, of work, and from lesson plans. To a large degree, what sporting activity is to be taught will have been decided at a school and

Was volleyball the best activity to develop teamwork?

What other affective traits could I have introduced using volleyball?

Did the children understand that successful volleyball play depends on teamwork?

Could I have introduced a cooperative concept in the pairs practice?

Does volleyball have any cultural significance that I could have used?

FIGURE 4.3 Subject matter

departmental level. However, you will need to ask questions about the appropriateness of certain activities for developing specific social and personal characteristics. So, although you might not have control of what is taught, in terms of activity, you will be able to determine what affective objectives you hope to achieve using that activity.

Did I pay as much attention to the girls as I did to the boys?

Did the less skilled get enough practice?

Do I always structure a competitive element into my lessons?

Harry seemed to be embarrassed about partnering a girl, why?

Could I have paired them up more fairly?

When I talk about Wimbledon and tennis clubs, does that make the poorer pupils feel uncomfortable?

FIGURE 4.4   Social and political issues

The last two topics for a reflective focus are probably the two most important. Teaching is supposed to be apolitical and socially just, so why should we ask ourselves questions about *social and political issues* (Figure 4.4)? For just that reason – to ascertain that our teaching really is equitable, non-élitist, fair, politically neutral and socially just. A wealth of critical theory literature confirms that any curriculum is politically and socially constructed within the context of the society in which it operates. There cannot be much argument about that. The point of this reflective topic is to eliminate the bias of that construction, or to counter it in overt ways instead of acquiescing to the covert process that perpetuates it.

Was I 'on form' today?

Did my enthusiasm for sports show through?

I seem to be directing operations all the time, is this OK?

Should I allow my pupils more autonomy in their decision making?

I always seem to structure my lessons in the same way – warm-up, practice, small game, full game. There must be a better/different way.

How can I encourage moral decision making in game play?

Do I encourage cheating/off-task by ignoring transgressions?

FIGURE 4.5   The practice of teaching

The *practice of teaching* (Figure 4.5) is different from the subject matter and teaching strategies. It relates more to a teaching style, a personal interpretation of what teaching is. It is concerned with how we structure our lessons, how much autonomy we give to our pupils and what messages we give out to our pupils in our practice of teaching. The way we appear, the role that we play and model, and the feelings and emotions that we demonstrate are all part of our practice of teaching. The technical side of teaching also needs to be considered. We must make sure that our practices are educationally sound. This category of reflective focus therefore covers a large range of elements.

The questions listed earlier under each of the focus topics should be viewed as starting points that can be used to trigger off other ideas and questions. Some of them will naturally lead to follow-up questions that are more probing and productive. In some cases, these questions will be replaced by a completely different set because the reflection is aimed at addressing a particular problem or issue. This questioning technique can be used in journal writing, as shown next, or with a 'critical friend', or in personal, individual reflection. Some examples of how this can work are described here.

Journal Writing

Journal writing has been extensively used in the USA as a way of getting children in schools to record and organise their thoughts about physical education. Attitudes, feelings and values can be discovered in this way. One of the problems with this method of data collection is that it impinges on valuable lesson time, a very contentious issue in England and Wales at the present time. Therefore, if journal writing were to be used for school pupils, it would need to be used sparingly and with a very fine focus. On the other hand, students, student teachers and beginning teachers may well find that keeping a reflective journal is helpful to them in their quest for professional development and their progress towards being a truly reflective practitioner.

Hedlund (1990) used journals and seminars with her students in the USA. She found that subsequent seminars with the student teachers were far more productive because the students had thought about the topics beforehand. To focus the comments, students were asked to address questions in their reflections. Questions such as 'What is fair?', 'Who is responsible for fairness in lessons?' and 'Is fairness the same as sportsmanship?' prompted open and thoughtful discussions.

The majority of student teachers and newly qualified teachers evaluate their lessons. Some will use a pro-forma outline to organise their evaluation and others will develop their own methods of recording and commenting on their lessons. A suggestion to promote the awareness of personal and social development in pupils is for formal evaluations to be suspended for a number of lessons and replaced with a reflective journal. Journal entries and seminar discussions with students can then be led in any direction by setting a relevant question to be addressed. For example, a student teaching a six-week unit on social and cultural dance could be asked to write a reflective journal instead of lesson evaluations. Student teachers could look specifically at social development by addressing such questions as 'Can you promote social behaviour while teaching dance?', 'In what ways do your pupils interact socially during dance lessons?'and 'How do your pupils react to an increased emphasis on sociability?' Seminars with the students on their return from teaching practice would then be very productive because they would all have given considerable thought to some of the affective elements in their teaching of physical education. The example journal entry shown in Figure 4.6 is the sort of thing the student or NQT could produce in the 'social dance' situation. It includes objectives, evidence and some reflection on the success of the lesson. Importantly, it also includes a suggestion for future action. Future journal entries would obviously comment on how the new strategy had worked out.

The questions in the example journal entry refer specifically to dance, but to broaden the subsequent discussions generic questions could be set. For example, 'Describe and comment on the social interaction that takes place in your lessons', 'Why do you think some pupils are reluctant to take part in competition?' and 'How did you plan for pupil enjoyment?' Students who had discussed these questions in relation to differing activities would bring a wealth of experience, thought and valuable information to seminar discussions.

Formal lesson evaluation can still be maintained in other units, but the addition of reflective journal writing and guided, meaningful discussion in seminars encourages the development of truly independent, reflective practitioners.

A 'Critical Friend'

It would be wrong to think that reflective practice is too introspective and insular. In fact, one of the most beneficial ways in which reflection can occur is by using a 'critical friend'. Although we are analysing our own practice in depth, we can do this in a collaborative way. This concept is explained well by David Kirk in the case study at the end of this chapter. It is self-evident that such a 'critical friend' must be an individual who is trusted and respected. This implies that the 'critical friend' must have a certain status and a level of knowledge, and that this individual also must have demonstrated a high level of teaching competency. Reflection using a 'critical friend' works best when that person is a 'master teacher' as well as a colleague.

Journal Sheet *(social development during dance unit)*

Class: *Yr 7, class xyz*

Date: *29 June 2000*

1 Brief lesson description.

What were the main objectives and themes of your lesson?

Improve working in mixed groups, boys with girls.

2 List evidence of pupil development.

All groups had boys and girls.

Five out of seven groups worked well together, no complaints.

Two groups argued – boys wouldn't really participate with girls.

3 How did it go, what would you change, how would you change it?

Explain and explore the things you stated in your evidence.

I'm disappointed by the two groups.

The boys see the dance lessons as 'girly'.

All boys together and all girls together defeats the object.

I know HOD plays rugby and the England rugby team use dance in their training, I think I'll ask him to team teach a dance session with me as a rugby training session – see how it goes.

FIGURE 4.6　Example of a journal entry

If others are used in the reflection process, such as with a 'critical friend', then the environment in which the reflection takes place should be safe, supportive and non-judgemental. Teachers doing this for the first time need to feel comfortable with surroundings and personnel. A crowded staffroom at lunchtime is probably not the best time or place to have a first attempt at being reflective! It is best to set aside a separate time when there will be no distractions or disturbances. A department office after regular school hours, or even at home, would be better than the busy period of preparation before school begins in the morning.

Teachers who decide to become reflective practitioners will have a good idea of what direction they want their reflection to go in. It may come about as a result of a critical incident in class, or a desire to try a new strategy. As mentioned earlier, one of the ways to begin the reflective process is to problematise a particular aspect of teaching and use that as a focus for reflection. In this way, the reflection and the questions asked will be self-directed. This is very closely related to the action research concept. However, if this process stalls, it is the role of the 'critical friend' to pose challenging and appropriate questions.

The reflective practitioner engages in a dialogue with him or herself. They ask the question and provide the answer. This process sometimes needs encouragement. The 'critical friend' can provide the impetus to continue the dialogue, or enable the subject to see connections between questions, answers and actions. Similarly, the friend should be able to probe into the detail, and perhaps ask more difficult questions on the subject's behalf. The friend should, at all times, refrain from giving the answers. Assisted self-reflection is akin to guided discovery for adults.

This hypothetical account between Tom the Teacher (TT) and his 'critical friend' (CF) after a Year 7 soccer lesson on dribbling shows how this type of aided reflection might unfold.

TT: I'm trying to be fair in my lessons and give everyone the same chance. I suppose I should ask myself if I achieved that in my last lesson.

CF: Seems like a good idea to me!

TT: Well, I managed to give every child some feedback or at least some recognition, I made a real effort to do that.

CF: So everyone received some of your attention. That's good. Did you do anything else?

TT: Er, yeah, they all played the same number of games and had the same number of practice goes.

CF: Good, tell me about the 'kick away' drill that you did at the beginning.

TT: Oh that, yeah, I thought it would be a good idea to put the skill under a bit of competitive stress – you know like in a real situation.

CF: Who were the most successful pupils?

TT: The better skilled players obviously!

CF: So who got the most practice?

TT: Like I said, the better skilled ones.

CF: What did the others do after they'd been eliminated?

TT: Just sat on the side. (pause) Oh, I see! the ones who needed the most practice didn't get it, and the ones who didn't really need the extra practice stayed in.

CF: That's what I saw. Now how could you change that to make it so that the less able got the same practice?

TT: But I don't want to lose the competitive bit.

CF: I don't think you have to – there must be a way around it.

TT: Well, instead of just sitting down they could carry on practising, maybe in the next grid.

CF: And where would you be?

TT: I'd have to look at both groups.

CF: But who would get most of your teaching attention?

TT: Well, I guess it makes sense for those who need the help, to get what they need. The good guys don't really need my feedback in that practice, just some recognition that they're doing OK.

CF: Yep, that would work. Now, what message did it send to those kids to be sitting down watching the better players?

TT: Yeah, right! They're not good enough to play, they're better off as spectators, they're not valued. But I didn't mean that to come across.

CF: Well, it wasn't that obvious, but I just put myself in their position. What do you think they were thinking?

TT: Probably, 'Oh, no! Out again. Harry's still in, I'll bet he wins, he always does. I'm just hopeless at this.'

CF: Probably.

TT: Wow, I didn't see it that way, thanks for telling me.

CF: Actually, you just told yourself!

Individual Reflection

Such a dialogue cannot take place when one is alone. However, if the reflective process has been progressive, you will have learned the questioning techniques and can almost be your own 'critical friend'. The principles are still the same. Problematise an area of practice, question and probe for truly reflective responses, and then act on those answers. This is a high-level, advanced teaching skill. Teachers who can operate in this manner will have progressed professionally to a point where they are undoubtedly intellectual practitioners, as opposed to technicians. Such a self-questioning attitude could be seen as insecurity, but in reality, the opposite is true. To put oneself in a vulnerable situation, by questioning one's own teaching, requires a great deal of strength of conviction. One is saying in effect, 'I know that I'm a good teacher, but I still want to be better. I'm going to examine my practice to see if I can find a way to improve my teaching. If this process highlights problems, then – Good; I can set about changing what I do to get even better.' This state of continual self-improvement should be the ultimate aim of all teachers who engage in the reflection process.

If, as is now becoming the case, teachers are to be assessed and rewarded according to the results of that assessment, then the reflective process described here could be instrumental in providing evidence to support that assessment. The aim, as already mentioned, must surely be to be more than just 'acceptable' as a teacher. Payment by results can be a powerful motivator, and teachers who indulge in reflective practice are undoubtedly better placed to progress beyond the 'acceptable'.

A CASE STUDY: REFLECTIVE PRACTICE AND ACTION RESEARCH

It has already been pointed out that reflective practice and action research are inextricably entwined. Teachers attempting to improve their practice must reflect on that practice. The study described here is a fine example of action research and reflective practice. It records the progress of a student teacher attempting to implement a 'gender equitable' Touch rugby programme in an Australian school (Kirk, 1995).

Doing Action Research in Physical Education: An Example
(Reproduced with permission from the *Journal of Sport Pedagogy*)

Sally was completing a teacher education programme. She was required to undertake an action research project over a 15-week period in a school of her choice on any topic she felt was of key importance to her own teaching of physical education. The action researchers were Sally, myself and Mike, one of the regular teachers in the school and Sally's school supervisor. Both Sally and Mike worked with a class of 25 14-year-old boys and girls on a games unit over the 15-week period. I adopted the role of critical friend, which meant that I was used by Sally and Mike as a source of suggestions, information, constructive criticism and encouragement. This role was consistent with my supervisory responsibilities as the university lecturer coordinating students' research projects.

Kemmis and McTaggart's Action Research Cycle

Sally's action research project took the approach developed by Kemmis and McTaggart (1982), who outline practical procedures for carrying out action research which are detailed and systematic, but are also flexible and adaptable. Sally used the four 'moments' of action research, proposed by Kemmis and McTaggart, of planning, acting, monitoring and reflecting, to structure her activities. The action research cycle is outlined as follows:

Planning: General idea
              Reconnaissance
              Field action
              First action step
              Monitoring
              Timetable
Acting: Implementation of the first action step
Monitoring: Collect data in the process of monitoring the first action step
Reflecting: Analyse what happened and construct the revised plan

Sally's Project: Initial Planning

Kemmis and McTaggart suggest that action research should be organised around a general idea which is shared by the participants and becomes the theme of the action research project. In a curriculum studies unit during the previous year of her programme, Sally had been impressed by an article by Helen Waite (1985) called 'Playing a different game: Towards a counter-sexist strategy in physical education and sport'. Waite argues that school programmes actively turn girls away from physical education and sport because they are made up of male-orientated activities. So, according to Waite, there need to be different forms of school physical education which are gender-sensitive. Sally discussed this issue with Mike and myself on a number of occasions prior to the start of the project, and we felt that its importance made it a suitable topic for Sally's project.

We decided together that the question of equal involvement and participation of boys and girls in the same game of Touch should form the *general idea* and theme of the project. (Touch is a non-contact form of rugby.) Sally began the planning phase of the project by attempting to write a few paragraphs about this general idea. I suggested that she retain a copy of what she had written to see if her ideas had changed by the end of the project. At this early stage Sally wanted to find out whether 'I treat girls and boys equally and what effect this has on girls' interest in playing Touch'. Sally said she thought her own teaching was sensitive to girls' experiences, and did not accept, at the beginning of her project, Waite's claim that physical education activities needed to be radically reformed. Instead, she believed it was up to the teacher to treat boys and girls equally.

Next, Sally together with Mike began a *reconnaissance* exercise as part of the planning process. This involved making sure that equipment and playing areas would be available when required. Sally also spent some time looking at the school physical education and sport policy. She was surprised to learn that the girls and boys in this school had been playing games together for only two years. Even now, not all games were coeducational, with girls being excluded from rugby football. Field hockey, netball and basketball were played by boys and girls, but as single-sex activities. Sally questioned Mike about this policy. He said that it had been initiated by the physical education staff, but only in face of fierce opposition from some parents who were concerned that their daughters might be injured.

Sally had decided that the *field of action* would be a class of 14-year-old girls and boys learning to play Touch. Next she and Mike had to decide what her *first action step* should be. Both felt that she needed to have some basic information on how they interacted with the students. They decided to videotape four lessons. Mike videotaped Sally teaching two Touch lessons and then Sally videotaped Mike teaching two lessons. They were especially interested in whether there was any difference in how they talked to boys and girls, and decided to count the number and type of their verbal interactions with pupils. This *monitoring* would supply initial information on their teaching. Sally and Mike also decided in discussions with me in my role as critical friend to keep a diary of their reactions to, and feelings about, the lessons. They planned to discuss these diary entries periodically during the reflection phases of the cycle. This information took two weeks to collect and was followed by a two-hour reflection session during which we watched parts of the videotapes together and Sally and Mike read out sections from their diaries.

Reflection no. 1

Sally thought she had spent an even amount of time interacting with boys and girls. However, the videotape revealed that about 40 per cent of her comments were directed to boys and another 40 per cent directed to the whole class. Around 30 per cent of Mike's comments were to boys and another 50 per cent to the entire class. Over half of Sally's verbal interactions were reprimands or what Siedentop calls 'desists' (Siedentop, 1983: 100). Sally was shocked and surprised at these results, as she sincerely believed that she talked more to girls than to boys and that her comments were mostly positive.

Sally and Mike then decided to look more closely at the tapes to see if they could explain what was going on in the lessons to produce these results. On close examination of the tapes, it was clear that the boys tended more often than the girls to make regular physical contact with each other and with the girls, such as pushing and bumping and in some cases knocking others over, or behaving in physically intimidating ways by waving their arms around and yelling, even though the rules of the game did not permit this. The girls generally, with only two exceptions, tended not to receive the ball often or else passed it quickly before anyone else could come near them. The boys also seemed to dominate the skill practice parts of the lessons, and it was obvious that some girls adopted what has been described as the 'competent bystander' strategy. In Sally's lessons there were more frequent stoppages for infringements of rules than in Mike's. Indeed, Mike had commented in his diary that he thought 'Sally should let the game flow more'. For her part, Sally was extremely frustrated that the girls would not participate more fully. It seemed to Sally that her verbal interactions with boys, many of which were desists, might be accounted for by their boisterous behaviour, which, as noted in her diary, 'is inappropriate in a co-ed game'.

As we talked about the lessons, Mike commented that the boys were only playing the way they had been used to playing other games, especially rugby. He said the boys' behaviour was 'natural'. He accepted, though, that the girls seemed to be given less opportunities to practise skills and participate in the games. Sally thought she had tried to encourage the girls with positive comments. However, even though she felt she was consciously trying to be sensitive to the girls' experiences, the videotapes showed that she tended to use boys much more often than girls to give demonstrations. We also noted that in skill practices, the boys and girls tended to form single-sex groups, and Sally had been hesitant about intervening to change this during the first two lessons she taught.

Revised Plan no. 1

Two considerations emerged from these reflections, which were to form the basis of a revised plan. First, Sally decided that both she and Mike should modify the rules of the game so that rough play, physical contact and intimidating behaviour were penalised by awarding a turn-over to the other team. They also decided to introduce a rule that the boys could only pass to a girl, while the other girls could pass to either another girl or a boy. This was made relatively easy to work out in practice since, in Touch, players pass down a line in regular play. In broken play, the girls had to make themselves available for a pass from a boy and so their participation became vital to the continuity and ultimate success of the game.

They decided to try this for two lessons which Sally would teach. Since the class was moving on to deal with tactics such as support play and making space for an overlap, both Sally and Mike felt it might not be difficult to put this rule to meaningful work in structuring the game. A second consideration which emerged from reflection was that during skill practice sessions, groups had to have an even balance of boys and girls. This new form of organising practice sessions was also to be trialled for two lessons.

Reflection no. 2

A week later, Sally wrote in her diary that these 'two lessons are the worst I have ever taught'. When we viewed the videotape of these two lessons, it was apparent that the boys were not prepared to accept the new rules, and continued to challenge Sally when she stopped the games for infringements of the physical contact rule, or the requirement that a boy should pass to a girl. Since Sally was determined to continue to see her plan through to the completion of the two lessons, some of the boys became reluctant to cooperate in the games and engaged in considerable off-task behaviour. The girls, on the other hand, seemed to be confused about their new levels of involvement in the game, and some clearly took a while to realise that their participation was now required if the game was to work successfully. One of the consequences of this mixture of confusion and reluctance from pupils was that Sally's verbal interactions with the pupils were even more negative than they had been in her first two lessons. We also noted that there was more than usual bickering among the pupils themselves, including name calling and put-downs.

Revised Plan no. 2

At this point Sally did not know what she should do next. Mike suggested that she separate pupils into single-sex groups for a few lessons, and then try them together again. Both Sally and I felt this would rather defeat the purpose of the project. Then he suggested that they try some team-teaching, so that he and Sally would have smaller groups to work with in the skill practice sessions. This seemed to offer some hope, although Sally could not see how it would improve pupils' conduct during the game. She reluctantly decided that perhaps she should persist with her plan of modifying the rules to penalise physical contact and to bring girls more into the game. She and Mike also decided that they would try to use only constructive positive verbal feedback with pupils, with an emphasis on encouragement for pupils who were performing well, especially the girls.

Reflection no. 3

Sally and Mike both felt that working with smaller groups in the skill practice sessions had worked well, and analysis of their verbal interactions with pupils showed a definite improvement in terms of proportion of verbal engagements with girls and boys, and in terms of positive feedback. However, as soon as pupils moved into playing a game, the same problems from the previous lessons began to emerge, with the boys refusing to cooperate with the new rules and girls remaining confused about their new role, although there was evidence from the video that some of the girls were beginning to get more involved.

Revised Plan no. 3

Sally was encouraged by this, but once again did not know what to try next. She and Mike thought they would continue with the same plan as the previous two lessons and work harder on their positive verbal interaction with pupils. However, between the reflection session and the next lesson, Sally attended a demonstration of a new game called Korfball at the university. This is a court game, a bit like netball, which is mixed sex and which explicitly rewards cooperative behaviour among players. Sally decided to revise her plan again and to incorporate some of the ideas of Korfball into her next two lessons.

Reflection no. 4

Sally had decided to award points for cooperative behaviour during the Touch games, and to subtract points for aggressive or uncooperative behaviour. The effect on the games was marked, and at our next reflection meeting Sally was excited. She felt that at last the boys were beginning to realise that they had to play differently in this activity, while the girls were gaining some confidence in their right to participate fully. Mike, surprisingly, was sceptical. After viewing the videotape, he commented that the boys were playing as if they had 'strait-jackets on'. He said that their play was 'stilted and unnatural'.

Revised Plan no. 4

Sally was undeterred by his comments, however, and decided to persist with this new approach until the end of the unit. Mike agreed with her that it would be appropriate to dispense with the video camera but to continue to audiotape Sally's verbal interactions. They also decided to give pupils some written work at the end of the three remaining lessons, which would provide an opportunity for them to say how they felt about playing Touch this way. Sally would also revert to taking the whole class by herself, with Mike making some detailed notes about pupils' positional play in the games and advising them and Sally about tactical improvements.

Of course, this is very much a tidied up and summarised account of Sally's action research project. Inadequate though this account is in terms of capturing the complexity of action research, I suggest that it does illustrate how Sally was able to develop some technical competencies of teaching (particularly those relating to her verbal interactions with pupils and the uses of positive reinforcement), her growing understanding and awareness of some physical education activities (particularly the gendered nature of games and sports and the different experiences boys and girls bring to playing games), and some ways in which she could change practices to challenge and redress social injustices (such as restructuring Touch to provide more opportunities for girls' participation and also challenging some boys' views on how games had to be played).

For Sally, the experience was in some respects a revelation, and she was very excited and encouraged by her ability to overcome adversity, as she saw it, and bounce back with some constructive solutions which worked. Looking back on her initial concern to treat pupils equally, Sally wrote in her diary that she now saw this approach as rather naïve and insufficient. Mike, on the other hand, thought that the new rules worked only because the boys were forced to behave 'unnaturally', even though he admitted that many of the girls in the class did become much more involved in the games and played at a level he did not think they were capable of. However, he did not think any of the boys in the group would change permanently the way they played.

This sort of ambiguous outcome is not uncommon with action research. As the least experienced teacher in the project 'team', Sally's eyes were opened to a new range of possibilities in physical education, and she was encouraged and invigorated by this. Mike, a hardened veteran of eight years of teaching, had seen some female students he regarded as unmotivated become highly involved in physical education lessons, but he remained sceptical about the longer-term benefits. And I had learned much from each of these teachers and their pupils. In particular, I had the privilege of witnessing some interesting and innovative teaching but seen, once again, that there are considerable challenges in bringing about educational reform in physical education at local level.

This case study clearly demonstrates a number of points. First, that success is not guaranteed; Sally had to persevere with her reflections and revised plans before she was able to see some progress. Secondly, reflection must be focused or it becomes diversified and random. And thirdly, inspiration can come from a number of sources. The idea to introduce elements of another game (Korfball) into the lessons came from Sally, not from her supervising teacher or from her critical friend.

In this example, there is evidence that the reflective process in the action research project was beginning to produce a more equitable form of physical education, at least for the girls in the group, although there were still questions to be addressed concerning Mike's worries about the inhibited play of the boys. It is also quite clear that this teacher had developed professionally as a result of the process. The ability to be a reflective practitioner carries many benefits for children, for teachers and for physical education programmes. (For a more complete account of reflective practice in physical education readers should look at Hellison and Templin, 1991.)

Conclusion

Although this book sets out to be a practical guide for teachers, it is hoped that teachers will use it as a resource rather than as a prescriptive document. It is something to be dipped into for ideas, not something to be followed word for word. In addition to the practical teaching strategy suggestions, I have included a brief look at the theory behind the notion of affective development through physical education.

It is a secondary purpose of this book to raise awareness of the vast potential of physical education. It is a subject that offers unique opportunities for physical, cognitive, social and affective development in pupils. It can contribute in a very real way to a truly holistic education. At the moment this potential is underused and the subject is undervalued. The realisation of the full potential would contribute greatly to an increase in the perceived educational worth of physical education, in turn raising the educational status, not only of the subject, but also of all its participants.

It has been well documented that 'top-down' change has very little effect on real-life practice. For example, the NCPE has not really changed the practice of physical education teaching in schools (Curtner-Smith, 1996). Good teachers are still teaching in much the same way, and schools are offering a range of activities similar to the range that was offered before the NCPE. This book is an attempt to instigate some 'bottom-up' change. This type of change has much more chance of influencing teaching in our schools because teachers themselves are involved in the change. The central element in this type of change is that teachers must believe in what they are teaching and how they are teaching it.

In terms of the curriculum, teachers have very little influence on what they are required to teach. Many believe in what they teach and many regard physical education as valuable, but personal involvement is not sufficiently invested in the curriculum to take teaching into the arena of meaningful commitment to the subject. By contrast, to make the ideas presented here work in real life, teachers must have a commitment to physical education in its entirety. Teaching is a social and personal act. This different approach recognises that fact and uses it as a strength.

By slightly changing the nature of the way we teach physical education, we can enable our subject to be a force for positive change and beneficial societal development. In adapting our teaching to take account of the potential for personal and social development through physical education, we will be making a contribution to the well-being of our pupils, to the growth in the potential of the education system and to the quality of our social and educational communities.

This force for positive change is not only the responsibility of teachers in schools. Institutions involved in teacher education must take account of these proposals and researchers must continue to investigate the teaching and learning process so that the new pedagogy can be developed into a body of knowledge. Academics are now attempting to 'understand' the curriculum rather than develop it. What do we understand by the fact that social responsibility and citizenship are very much on the curriculum? What does it mean that political literacy is viewed as a strand of citizenship? Although this different approach with its new pedagogy offers many opportunities and some answers, it also poses many questions. It is up to the community of educators to accept the challenge and investigate those questions.

What has been described and recommended here is a different approach to teaching physical education. It recognises the desirability of educating the whole person, not just easily categorised aspects of the person. Thus, it is not only the physical abilities of a pupil that will be developed with this approach; it is the social and personal, the affective elements of being that will benefit. This approach also recognises physical education as a school subject that has a number of domains, for example psychomotor, cognitive, social and affective. This eclectic, philanthropic pedagogy links the underused social and affective domains of the subject with the affective element of personal development, thus producing a harmonious, logical relationship between teacher, subject and learner. Development becomes individual and teaching and learning become relevant and contextual.

As we enter into a new era of human endeavour, and as a new millennium begins to unfold, the notion of postmodernism ought to begin to be applied to education. We live in a pluralist society, localised but with global tendencies. We have a scientific legacy that has provided us with much essential knowledge and we are beginning to realise the need to personalise learning, making it subjective, applicable and engaging. So we need to take the best of what there is, to reconstruct it into a relevant curriculum and to apply it to our practice. Learning in physical education needs to become individualised to make it meaningful to our pupils. What better way to make a subject meaningful than to use it to develop the whole person?

There are two major government initiatives, and a proposed application of educational theory, that support this new role for physical education. The new framework for PSHE (QCA, 1999a) and the citizenship theme (QCA, 1998) that are being incorporated into educational provision are huge opportunities for physical education to take the lead in offering itself as a perfect vehicle for these cross-curricular initiatives. The exposition of this opportunity is developed in *Beyond the Boundaries of Physical Education* (Laker, 2000). That theoretical framework is expanded into practical applications here, in this present book. These practical applications are especially pertinent now, but they will also stand the test of time and be relevant to future generations of teachers and students of physical education. Further political policy changes are unlikely to undo what is currently being expounded in political and educational arenas.

The educational theory that provides additional support is the notion of situated learning. This is part of the constructivist theory of learning that states that learners develop understanding and learning by integrating new knowledge with existing knowledge and assimilating the mix into a version of knowledge relevant to them and their particular contexts. Kirk and Macdonald (1998) apply this theory to physical education and propose that the location of the learning should be relevant, that teachers should lead pupils into a community of participants, and that participation should have meaning and purpose for the individuals concerned. The proposals outlined in these pages clearly meet these criteria. Learners will develop socially and personally by relating current experiences to previous experiences and by amalgamating the two into a developing affective dimension of themselves. Learning experiences are placed in relevant locations, that is they will learn about teamwork, for example, in situations that require teamwork. Children will become part of a community of learners, and sports participants, as they work together through the learning process. And lastly, by seeing that individual characteristics are targeted, it will be apparent that this learning is relevant to their own physical, social and personal development.

A number of forces in education seem to be coming together at an opportune time. Government and educational initiatives are supportive; our knowledge of the technical aspects of teaching is comprehensive; and we have an obligation to develop our learners as skilled, enthusiastic, social and responsible community members and citizens. It has been demonstrated that physical education and school sport have a major contribution to make in this regard. Perhaps this book will be the impetus for teachers to 'give it a go'. There is nothing to lose but a growing disaffection with physical education and a growing defection from sport and exercise. On the other hand, the research tells us that the gains that can be made are impressive. The benefits reach far beyond the individual; they reach as far as community and society. What better legacy for a school subject than to be instrumental in developing citizens and strengthening our various communities?

Appendices

The photocopiable sheets that follow – for a unit of work, a lesson plan and a journal page – can be used by teachers to develop their use of the new approach outlined in this book.

Appendix A: Blank Unit of Work

Area of activity:		Unit title:	
Key Stage:		Year:	

Lesson structure	Lesson 1	Lesson 2	Lesson 3
Introduction			
Development			
Conclusion			
Cross-curricular element			

Resources needed	Assessment criteria

Time (lessons × mins):		
Objectives:		
Lesson 4	Lesson 5	Lesson 6
	Cross-curricular teaching strategy	

Photocopiable
Resource

Appendix B: Blank Lesson Plan

Area of activity:		Key Stage:	
Unit title:		Length of lesson:	
Class:	Number:		Lesson:
Objectives:			

Time:	Activity	Organisation/equipment

Photocopiable
Resource

Year:
Equipment:

Teaching points/differentiation	Cross-curricular elements

Appendix C: Blank Journal Page

Class: _____

Date: _____

Journal sheet

1 **Brief lesson description.** What were the main objectives and themes of your lesson?

[   ]

2 **List evidence of pupil development.**

[   ]

3 **How did it go, what would you change, how would you change it?**
Explain and explore the things you stated in your evidence.

[   ]

References

BALL, S. (1995) 'Intellectuals or technicians? The urgent role of theory in educational studies', *British Journal of Educational Studies*, 43 (3), 255–71.

CAPEL, S., LEASK, M. and TURNER, T. (eds) (1995) *Learning to teach in the secondary school: A companion to school experience*, London: Routledge.

CARLSON, J.B. (1982) 'How do you measure a rainbow? Assessment of the affective', *Viewpoints*, EDRS document (227 088).

CARROLL, B. (1994) *Assessment in physical education: A teacher's guide to the issues*, London: Falmer Press.

CASBON, C. (1999) 'Teaching and learning in physical education', Paper presented at 'Getting education back into physical education', a seminar for physical education teachers and teacher educators, Durham, UK.

COMMISSION FOR FAIR PLAY (1990) *Fair play for kids*, Gloucester, Ontario: Commission for Fair Play.

COMPAGNONE, N. (1995) 'Teaching responsibility to rural elementary youth: Going beyond the urban at-risk boundaries', *Journal of Physical Education, Recreation and Dance*, 66 (6), 58–63.

CURTNER-SMITH, M.D. (1996) 'The impact of the National Curriculum on secondary school physical education: A case study in one English town', in LAKER, A., CURTNER-SMITH, M.D. and CLARKE, G. *Physical education within the National Curriculum in England and Wales: Some ideas for the United States (Symposium)*, National AAHPERD Convention, Atlanta, Georgia.

CUTFORTH, N. and PARKER, M. (1996) 'Promoting affective development in physical education: The value of journal writing', *Journal of Physical Education, Recreation and Dance*, 67 (7), 19–23.

DARST, P. W., ZAKRAJSEK, D. B. and MANCINI, V.H. (1989) *Analyzing physical education and sport instruction*, Champaign, IL: Human Kinetics.

DEPARTMENT FOR EDUCATION (1995) *Physical Education in the National Curriculum (Statutory Orders)*, London: Her Majesty's Stationery Office.

GIBBONS, S. L. and EBBECK, V. (1997) 'The effect of different teaching strategies on the moral development of physical education students', *Journal of Teaching in Physical Education*, 17 (1), 85–98.

GIBBONS, S.L., EBBECK, V. and WEISS, M.R. (1995) 'Fair play for kids: Effects on the moral development of children in physical education', *Research Quarterly for Exercise and Sport*, 66 (2), 247–55.

GIEBINK, M.P. and McKENZIE, T.L. (1985) 'Teaching sportsmanship in physical education and recreation: An analysis of interventions and generalization effects', *Journal of Teaching in Physical Education*, 4 (3), 167–77.

GRINESKI, S. (1993) 'Achieving educational goals in physical education – A missing ingredient', *Journal of Physical Education, Recreation and Dance*, 64 (5), 32–4.

HARTER, S. (1985) *Manual for the self-perception profile for children*, Colorado: University of Denver.

HEDLUND, R. (1990) 'Non-traditional team sports – taking full advantage of the teachable moment', *Journal of Physical Education, Recreation and Dance*, 61 (4), 76–9.

HELION, J. G. (1996) 'If we build it, they will come. Creating an emotionally safe physical education environment', *Journal of Physical Education, Recreation and Dance*, 67 (6), 40–4.

HELLISON, D. R. (1985) *Goals and strategies for teaching physical education*, Champaign, IL: Human Kinetics.

HELLISON, D.R. and TEMPLIN, T.J. (1991) *A reflective approach to teaching physical education*, Champaign, IL: Human Kinetics.

JEWETT, A.E. and BAIN, L.L. (1985) *The curriculum process in physical education*, Dubuque, IA: Wm. C. Brown Publishers.

JOURNAL OF PHYSICAL EDUCATION, RECREATION AND DANCE (1993) 64 (5).

KEMMIS, S. and McTAGGART, R. (1982) *The action research planner*, 2nd edn, Geelong: Deakin University Press.

KEMMIS, S. and McTAGGART, R. (1988) *The action research planner*, 3rd edn, Geelong: Deakin University Press.

KIRK, D. (1986) 'A critical pedagogy for teacher education: Towards an inquiry-oriented approach', *Journal of Teaching in Physical Education*, 5 (4), 236–46.

KIRK, D. (1995) 'Action research and educational reform in physical education', *Pedagogy in Practice*, 1 (1), 4–21.

KIRK, D. and MACDONALD, D. (1998) 'Situated learning in physical education', *Journal of Teaching in Physical Education*, 17 (3), 376–87.

LAKER, A. (2000) *Beyond the boundaries of physical education: Educating young people for citizenship and social responsibility*, London: RoutledgeFalmer.

LAMBERT, D. (1995) 'An overview of assessment: Principles and practice', in CAPEL, S., LEASK, M. and TURNER, T. (eds) *Learning to teach in the secondary school: A companion to school experience*, London: Routledge.

LEE, M. (ed.) (1993) *Coaching children in sport*, London: E. & F.N. Spon.

LUND, J. (1997) 'Authentic assessment, its developments and applications', *Journal of Physical Education, Recreation and Dance*, 68 (7), 25–8, 40.

MAWER, M. (1995) *The effective teaching of physical education*, London: Longman.

McHUGH, E. (1995) 'Going "beyond the physical": Social skills and physical education', *Journal of Physical Education, Recreation and Dance*, 66 (4), 18–21.

MOSSTON, M. and ASHWORTH, S. (1990) *The spectrum of teaching styles – from command to discovery*, New York: Longman.

NATIONAL CURRICULUM COUNCIL (NCC) (1990) *Curriculum guidance 3. The whole curriculum*, York: NCC.

PARKER, M., KALLUSKY, J. and HELLISON, D. R. (1999) 'High impact, low risk: Ten strategies to teach responsibility', *Journal of Physical Education, Recreation and Dance*, 70 (2), 26–8.

PHILLIPS, D. A. and CARLISLE, C. (1983) 'A comparison of physical education teachers categorized as most and least effective', *Journal of Teaching in Physical Education*, 2 (3), 55–67.

PHILLIPS, D. A., CARLISLE, C., STEFFEN, J and STROOT, S. (1986) 'The Physical Education Teacher Assessment Instrument: Computerised version', unpublished manuscript, Greeley, Colorado: University of Northern Colorado.

QUALIFICATIONS AND CURRICULUM AUTHORITY (QCA) (1998) *Final Report of the Advisory Group on Education for Citizenship and the Teaching of Democracy in Schools*, London: QCA.

QUALIFICATIONS AND CURRICULUM AUTHORITY (QCA) (1999a) *Education 3–16: A framework for personal, social and health education (PSHE) and citizenship at key stages 1 to 4*, London: QCA.

QUALIFICATIONS AND CURRICULUM AUTHORITY (QCA) (1999b) *The review of the National Curriculum in England: Consultation materials*, London: QCA.

QUALIFICATIONS AND CURRICULUM AUTHORITY (QCA) (1999c) *Physical Education. The National Curriculum*, London: QCA.

ROWE, J. (1995) 'The non-physical aims of physical education', unpublished special study, College of St Mark and St John, Plymouth.

SCHON, D.A. (1987) *Educating the reflective practitioner*, London: Jossey-Bass.

SCHOOL CURRICULUM AND ASSESSMENT AUTHORITY (SCAA) (1996) *A guide to the National Curriculum*, London: SCAA.

SHARPE, T.L., BROWN, M. and CRIDER, K. (1995) 'The effects of a sportsmanship curriculum intervention on generalized positive social behavior of urban elementary school students', *Journal of Applied Behavior Analysis*, 28 (4), 401–16.

SIEDENTOP, D. (1983) *Developing teaching skills in physical education*, 2nd edn, Palo Alto, CA: Mayfield Publishing Company.

SIEDENTOP, D. (1991) *Developing teaching skills in physical education*, 3rd edn, Mountain View, CA: Mayfield Publishing Company.

SIEDENTOP, D. (1994) *Sport education: Quality PE through positive sport experience*, Champaign, IL: Human Kinetics.

UNDERWOOD, G. (1983) *The physical education curriculum in the secondary school: Planning and implementation*, London: Falmer Press.

UNDERWOOD, M. and WILLIAMS, A. (1991) 'Personal and social education through gymnastics', *British Journal of Physical Education*, 22 (4), 15–19.

WAITE, H. (1985) 'Playing a different game: Towards a counter-sexist strategy in physical education and sport', *Education Links*, 25, 23–5.

WHITEHEAD, J.R. (1995) 'A study of children's physical self-perceptions using an adapted physical self-perception questionnaire', *Pediatric Exercise Science*, 7, 123–51.

ZEICHNER, K.M. and TABACHNICK, B.R. (1991) 'Reflections on reflective teaching', in TABACHNICK, B.R. and ZEICHNER, K.M. (eds) *Issues and practices in inquiry-oriented teacher education*, Philadelphia: Falmer Press.

Index